TWENTY PHILADELPHIA ARTISTS:

CELEBRATING FLEISHER *CHALLENGE* AT TWENTY

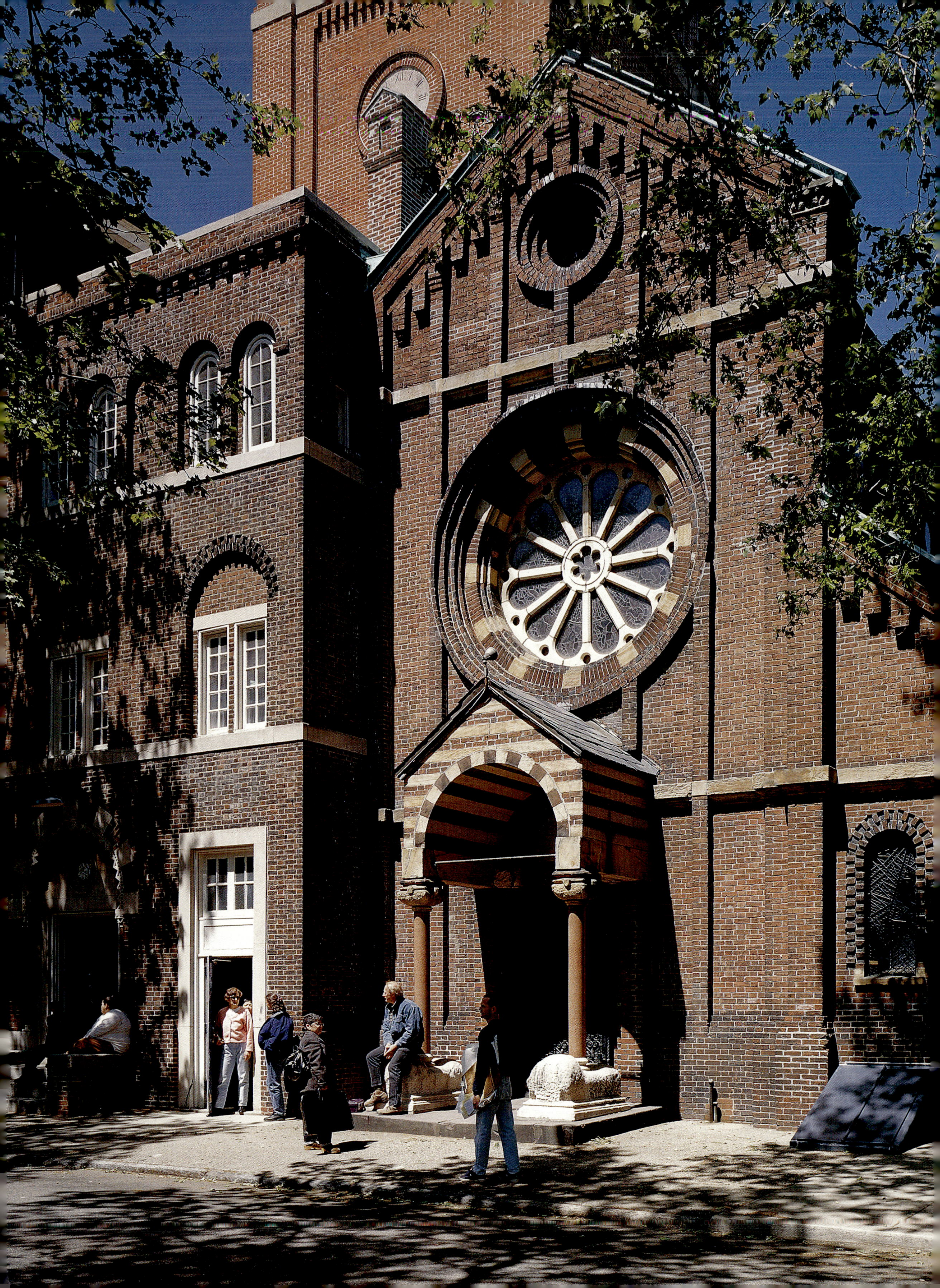

TWENTY PHILADELPHIA ARTISTS:

CELEBRATING FLEISHER *CHALLENGE* AT TWENTY

JOHN B. RAVENAL

With an essay by

THORA JACOBSON

PHILADELPHIA MUSEUM OF ART

**Published on the occasion of an exhibition at the
Philadelphia Museum of Art, July 18–September 13, 1998**

**A complementary invitational exhibition, *20 x 12: A Generation
of "Challenge" Artists*, surveying the work of 180 *Challenge*
participants, has been organized by the Samuel S. Fleisher Art
Memorial, Philadelphia, July 18–August 28, 1998.**

Cover: Detail of *Net of Indra* by Bruce Pollock (plate 17)
Frontispiece: Samuel S. Fleisher Art Memorial, 719 Catharine Street, Philadelphia

Editor: Sherry Babbitt
Designer: Bethany Johns Design
Production manager: Matthew Pimm
Printer: Meridian Printing, East Greenwich, Rhode Island
Color separator: Professional Graphics, Inc., Rockford, Illinois

Produced by the Department of Publications
Philadelphia Museum of Art
Benjamin Franklin Parkway at 26th Street
P.O. Box 7646
Philadelphia, Pennsylvania 19101-7646

Printed and bound in the United States of America

Library of Congress Cataloging-in-Publication Data
Ravenal, John B., 1959–
    Twenty Philadelphia artists : celebrating Fleisher Challenge at
twenty / John B. Ravenal ; essay by Thora Jacobson.
        p.   cm.
    Catalog of an exhibition held at the Philadelphia Museum of Art
July 18–Sept. 13, 1998.
    ISBN 0-87633-124-X (alk. paper)
    1. Art, American—Pennsylvania—Philadelphia—Exhibitions.
2. Art, Modern—20th century—Pennsylvania—Philadelphia—
Exhibitions. 3. Challenge (Exhibition). I. Jacobson, Thora.
II. Challenge (Exhibition). III. Philadelphia Museum of Art.
IV. Title.
    N6535.P5R38   1998
    709'.748'1107474811—dc21   98-23822
                                                           CIP

CONTENTS

FOREWORD

From the moment you enter the door of 719 Catharine Street in South Philadelphia, the inimitably congenial atmosphere of the Samuel S. Fleisher Art Memorial reaches out to embrace you. An unexpected and lively juxtaposition of spaces—including a cheerful and functional maze of studios and galleries, a Byzantine-revival sanctuary complete with a vast gilded altarpiece that Fleisher commissioned from his friend Violet Oakley, and a lecture room dedicated to Louis I. Kahn that is itself a work of art by Siah Armajani—instantly offers up the soul of the place. Devoted since its founding a century ago to the needs of artists, and blessed today with a dedicated and creative board and staff, Fleisher seems younger than ever.

For the Philadelphia Museum of Art, this exhibition is a two-fold pleasure to present. It celebrates the centenary of Fleisher and the twentieth anniversary of its creative *Challenge* exhibition program, and at the same time pays tribute to one of Philadelphia's most invaluable resources: its large and vital community of living artists. Fleisher's indefatigable Director, Thora Jacobson, who contributes her own perspective to this catalogue, is another Philadelphia treasure to be saluted. Our delight in this occasion is tempered only by our sadness over the imminent departure of John Ravenal, whose thoughtful eye has guided every stage of this project and earned him much respect and affection both inside and outside the Museum during his nearly seven-year tenure on the curatorial staff. We wish him the very best as he assumes his new role as Curator of Art After 1900 at the Virginia Museum of Fine Arts in Richmond, and are grateful that his last project for this Museum was this lively and timely exhibition, accomplished in such fine style.

Without the concerted and enthusiastic efforts of many staff members of both Fleisher and the Museum, this exhibition and its catalogue could not have been brought into being. We owe a great debt of thanks as well to the Pew Charitable Trusts and the William Penn Foundation for grants which ensured that both the presentation and publication of the exhibition could live up to their subject. We are most of all indebted to the artists themselves—20 of whom are shown here and their 228 colleagues who have exhibited in twenty years of *Challenge* shows—whose diversity of medium, style, and viewpoint has found common ground in greater Philadelphia over the past two decades. It is the artists who make this city and its surrounding region a thoroughly exciting place in which to encounter contemporary art at its most vital.

ANNE D'HARNONCOURT
The George D. Widener Director
and Chief Executive Officer

ANN TEMKIN
Muriel and Philip Berman Curator of
Twentieth-Century Art

ACKNOWLEDGMENTS

This exhibition and catalogue have offered me the pleasure of working closely with twenty artists who are or were based in the Philadelphia region and who share the distinction of having shown in the *Challenge* exhibition series at the Samuel S. Fleisher Art Memorial. First and foremost, I would like to thank each of these individuals. It has been a privilege to visit their studios and discuss their work with them over this past year. I also extend my appreciation to the some two hundred other *Challenge* artists whose work we considered through the many rounds of the selection process. It has been a pleasure to learn more about their work during this project. Our profound appreciation is also due to the many collectors who have generously made the works of these artists accessible to me during my research; many have also generously lent works to the exhibition.

To produce a museum exhibition and catalogue involves the expertise of numerous individuals working together toward a common goal. The choice of the twenty artists was made by a team that included Thora Jacobson, Director, and Warren Angle, Gallery Coordinator, from the Fleisher Art Memorial, and Ann Temkin, Curator of Twentieth-Century Art, and myself from the Museum. I am grateful to Thora, Warren, and Ann for their spirited collaboration and for their thoughtful feedback on my selection of works and my catalogue texts. We received helpful responses during the initial stages from Museum curators Dilys E. Blum, John Ittmann, Martha Mock, Ann Percy, Darrel L. Sewell, and Innis Howe Shoemaker, and from Alice O. Beamesderfer, who also coordinated many of the complex issues associated with the exhibition installation. I am grateful as well to Virginia Pye and Anne d'Harnoncourt for their comments on my text. Additional thanks are due to Thora for her catalogue essay, which so clearly describes the local cultural atmosphere in which the *Challenge* series was born and developed.

The exhibition and catalogue could not have been realized without the unfailingly enthusiastic support of my assistant, Kathleen Forde, with whom it has been a delight to work. I am also indebted to Sherry Babbitt of the Publications Department for her thorough and sensitive editing of the catalogue. Suzanne F. Wells and her assistant, Amanda Lutz, coordinated many aspects of the exhibition planning with their usual good cheer. I also extend my thanks to George H. Marcus and Matthew Pimm of the Publications Department; Elie-Anne Chevrier, Sara Detweiler, and Irene Taurins from the Registrar's Office; Linda Jacobs, Mari M. Jones, and Donna Rim for their fund-raising efforts;

Installation Technicians Sarah Boxer, James Grentzenberg, Don E. Kaiser, Martha Masiello, and Alane Salvatore; Installation Design Coordinator Jack Schlechter; Conservators Nancy Ash, P. Andrew Lins, Sally Malenka, Suzanne Penn, and Faith H. Zieske; and Photographers Lynn Rosenthal and Graydon Wood. Special thanks are due to Bethany Johns for her elegant design of the publication. I have been enormously gratified over my nearly seven years at the Philadelphia Museum of Art to work with such a dedicated and skilled group of people as this staff. In this regard, I especially appreciate the expansive vision, high standards, and sound judgment of Ann Temkin and Anne d'Harnoncourt, with whom it has been a privilege to work.

Working in Philadelphia has also afforded me the chance to take part in a rich and varied art scene, to which this exhibition pays tribute. For this project, we received gracious assistance in our research from Larry Becker and Heidi Nivling at Larry Becker Contemporary Art; John Ollman at Fleisher/Ollman Gallery; Becky Kerlin at Gallery Joe; J. Rudy Lewis, Sueyun Locks, and Philip Mott at Locks Gallery; Charles More and Saskia Nilsen at The More Gallery, Inc.; Brian Kibler and Rick Snyderman at Snyderman Gallery; and Michael Murphy, Megan Walborn, and Sande Webster at Sande Webster Gallery.

J B R

TWENTY ARTISTS FOR TWENTY YEARS

J O H N   B .   R A V E N A L

For the past twenty years, the Samuel S. Fleisher Art Memorial's *Challenge* exhibition series has provided an important showcase for both emerging and more established artists in the Philadelphia region. Nearly 250 artists, in four three-person shows each year,[1] have taken part since the inception of the series. Many of the area's finest artists count their *Challenge* exhibitions as pivotal experiences, offering them a place to be taken seriously as professionals and to take risks without the pressure of commercial success as the measure of artistic value. To be selected for one of the twelve exhibition slots from the more than three hundred yearly applicants is widely recognized as a significant achievement.

The *Challenge* series has welcomed a remarkably broad range of practice over its two decades. *Challenge* artists span every conceivable approach to making art, from those most faithful to tradition to those most resistant. The jurying process for the exhibition fosters this broad eclecticism. A team comprised of an established local artist and a local curator make the preliminary choices in each medium. The final selections are made in a second round by an all-artist interdisciplinary panel. The diversity of *Challenge* artists is also the natural outcome of the plurality of styles and approaches found in the Philadelphia area, and the series's twenty-year roster of artists provides telling insight into a generation of art-making in the region.

The Philadelphia Museum of Art has had a long affiliation with the Fleisher Art Memorial and the *Challenge* series. By instruction of Samuel S. Fleisher's will, the Museum originally administered Fleisher. While Fleisher now functions with an

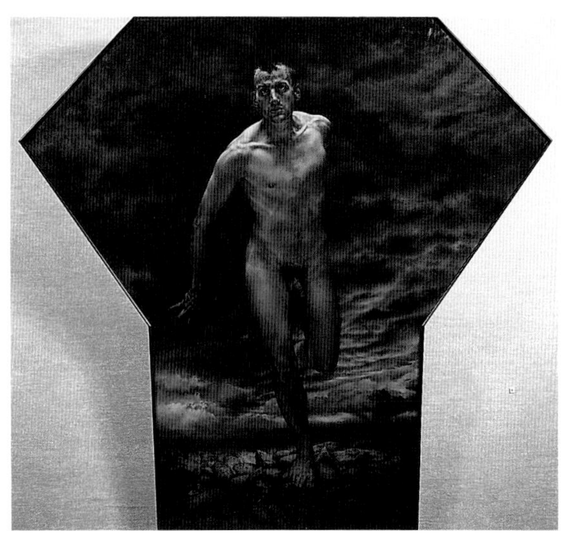

Lisa Bartolozzi
Fallen Angel, 1992
Oil on panel
86 × 86" (218.4 × 218.4 cm)
Collection of Lynn Herrick Sharp

autonomous board, the two institutions retain certain admini-strative connections. In addition, curators from many of the Museum's departments have often served as *Challenge* jurors.

In collaboration with the Fleisher staff, the Museum has organized the current exhibition to pay tribute to twenty years of *Challenge* exhibitions, an anniversary that coincides with Fleisher's centennial as a tuition-free art school. Selections for the Museum's exhibition were made with an eye toward creating a retrospective summary of the *Challenge* series. In an appropriate reflection of the diverse range of styles, mediums, and subjects of *Challenge* artists, included in the show are figurative painters working with Renaissance techniques and abstract painters work-ing with conceptual structures; ceramicists making sculpture and sculptors making installations; photographers scrutinizing the human body and printmakers working improvisationally.

The notion of "Philadelphia art" has long been associated with a particular figurative style, identified primarily with the Pennsylvania Academy of the Fine Arts, and, for much of the nineteenth century and throughout the first half of this one, the Academy's school and museum did have a dominant role in shaping the area's artistic profile. In the late 1970s, however, the emergence of the Fleisher *Challenge* series, along with the growth of the local cooperative and commercial gallery scene, played a part in the erosion of a cohesive regional style and helped foster the viability of pluralism in the region's contempo-rary art. The rise of such non-Academy venues was due in part to the increasing strength of other, long-established art schools and departments, including the Philadelphia College of Art (now the University of the Arts), the Moore College of Art and Design, the University of Pennsylvania, and the Tyler School of Art. This shift in the 1970s toward the coexistence of many styles locally reflects national and international trends of the period in which an increasingly rapid proliferation of styles and cross-pollenization among the offspring of Pop, Minimalism, and Conceptual art defeated once and for all the notion of a systematic progression of dominant styles. Nonetheless, among the broad range that characterizes art of the last twenty years in Philadelphia, there are significant shared themes and approaches, many of which can be traced in the eclectic group of artists in this show.

Artists have been actively extending and confounding the conventional distinctions between mediums for nearly forty years, beginning with Happenings, Fluxus, and Conceptual art. Artists in Philadelphia build on this healthy disregard for conventional limitations, but couple it with a respect for age-old forms, materials, and subjects. Lisa Bartolozzi, for example, who makes painstakingly realist images of the human figure using a Renaissance technique of applying layers of colored glazes, often presents her images on unusually shaped canvases or in architectural frames (figure 1). Stephen Talasnik combines virtuosic draftsmanship using the basics of drawing—charcoal and graphite—with subtractive, almost sculptural methods, including working the surface of his drawings with sandpaper, steel wool, and wire brushes (figure 2).

Artists in the exhibition working in photography also stretch the conventional boundaries of their medium, building on the photography-based innovations of their predecessors, including the Starn Twins and Jeff Wall. Norinne Betjemann bleaches and paints her images with photo oils and gold leaf, and sometimes encases them in solid resin. Gabriel Martinez has mounted some of his photographs on extension mirrors and others in unsealed light boxes, giving them an assertive, physical presence. Kate Moran pierces and scrapes her photographic negatives, and has sewn photographic prints together into quilts of images.

Three of the artists in the show, Moran, Brooke Moyer, and Mei-ling Hom, bring to other mediums the methods and approaches from their experience working with ceramics, including an embrace of labor-intensive processes, attention to carefully worked surfaces, and retention of the vessel as a basic concept—be it Moran's images of bodies as fragile vessels, Moyer's industrial/biological hybrids, or Hom's enclosures that serve as temporary containers or passageways for the body (figure 3). The two artists working exclusively in ceramics, Syd Carpenter and Don Nakamura, come to their medium from other disciplines and bring with them unconventional approaches. Carpenter began as a painter and eschews the glazing tradition;

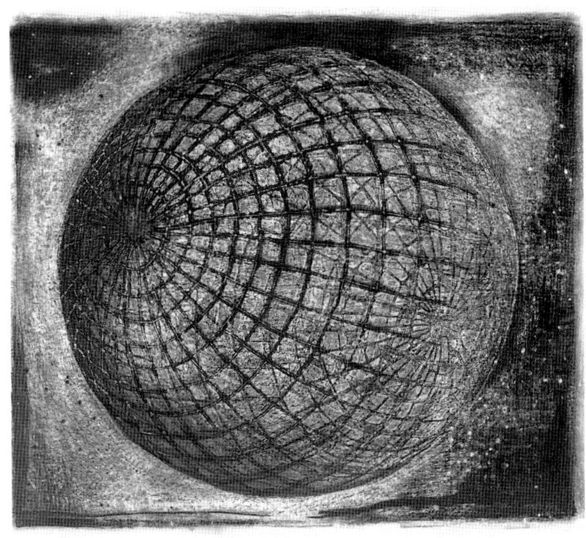

Stephen Talasnik
Mooring, 1993–94
Graphite on paper
34 × 38" (86.3 × 96.5 cm)
Collection of the artist

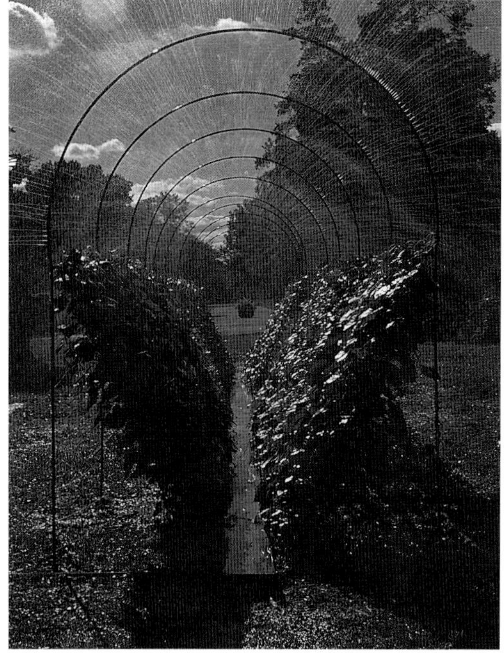

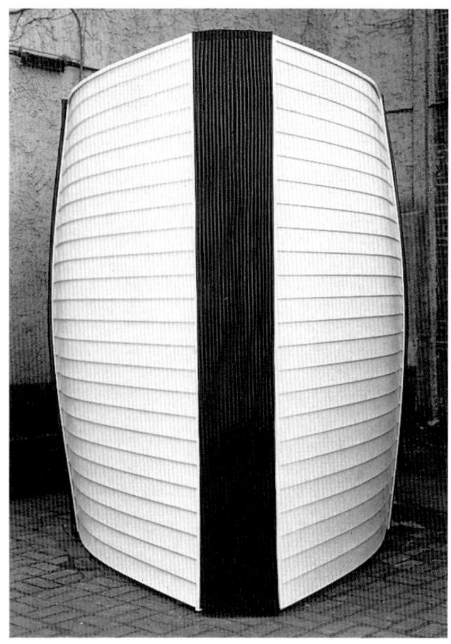

she instead paints her forms with acrylics after they are fired. Nakamura, on the other hand, originally studied music, as is evident in his additive and improvisational approach to hand-building and the jubilant rhythms of his glazing.

Installation art is a medium inherently resistant to traditional categorization. Often temporary by intention, installation art continues to some degree the resistance to making collectible objects that inspired its originators in the 1960s. Most commonly exploring extensions of sculptural issues but at times also embracing architecture, theater, and environmental art, installation is uniquely suited to respond to specific sites for which it is made. Mei-ling Hom, Tristin Lowe, and Michael Grothusen have each created new installations for the exhibition, affording them the chance to engage with aspects of the museum context.

An attitude of freedom toward the conventions of mediums has often inspired these artists' choice of everyday, nonart materials. Working near the end of a century-long process of incorporating vernacular culture into fine art, and coming of age on the heels of the experimental forms of the 1970s, artists over the last twenty years have felt it nearly their birthright to make art out of anything that suits their needs. Lanny Bergner, for example, makes sculpture with aluminum screening, fishhooks, and nylon stockings, whereas Michael Grothusen has used vinyl siding and the rubber accordion material found between double buses (figure 4). Mei-ling Hom's installations have included Asian spices, cooking utensils, and saplings of "invasive alien" species.

This flexibility and resourcefulness often reflect a conceptual approach in which an initial idea determines the form. But the precision and care that mark these artists' uses of everyday materials also reveal a concern with the formal possibilities of these materials that are often unexpected in light of their humble origins. Stacy Levy's installation *Seeing the Path of the Wind* (figure 5) incorporated weathervanes, electric fans, and a thousand tiny organza flags. Another of her installations, *Watercourse,* at the University of the Arts in Philadelphia in 1996, represented every one of the region's bodies of running water, both existing and lost, using eight thousand plastic cups filled and refilled with six tons of stream and river water. Her disciplined use of these ordinary objects in the ser-

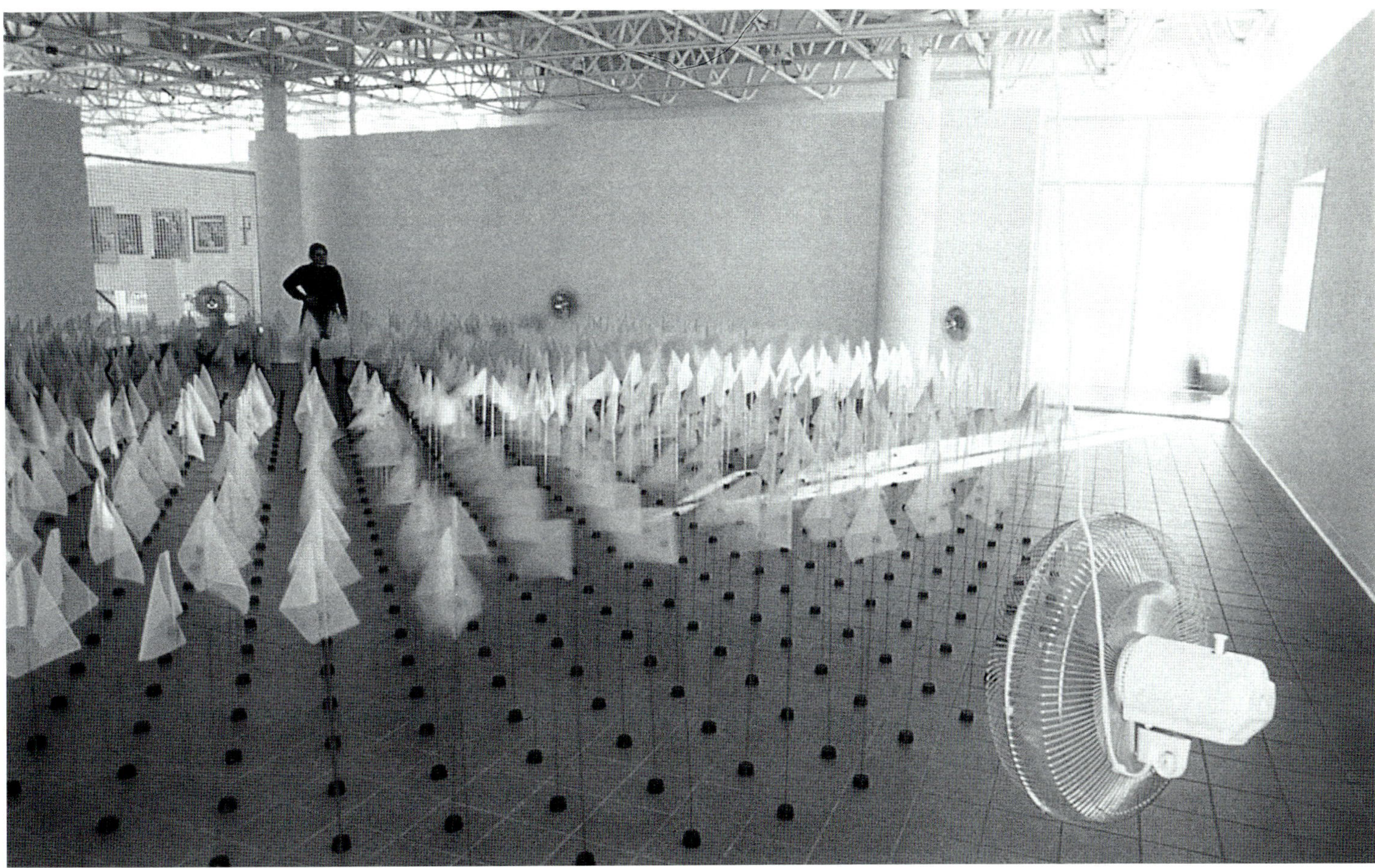

vice of her ideas recalls a scholar's felicitous description of
Conceptual artist Sol LeWitt's work as "the look of thought."[2]

Other artists using unconventional materials opt for a layering of complex and elusive meanings that is the very antithesis of
Levy's clarity. Tristin Lowe's installations have included mattresses
with fountains, plastic tents lit by bare bulbs, inflatable clown
dolls, wires, work lamps, and empty buckets (figure 6). His is a
raw aesthetic, as unsettling in its exposure of the mechanics as it
is surprising in the space it creates for the imagination. Stuart
Netsky uses a range of provocative substances to complicate an
already murky area where art, fashion, vanity, and mortality over-
lap. In a series of prints with titles such as *Obsession, Infinity,* and
Eternity (figure 7), he used ground-up AIDS pharmaceuticals,
applied as flocking on paper, to make pale, ghostlike re-creations
of the advertisements for these suggestively titled perfumes. He
has also remade famous works of art in vernacular and domestic
materials, turning Monet's *Wheatstacks* and *Water Lilies* into
flickering billboards (plate 16) and Barnett Newman's exemplar
of mid-twentieth-century abstract painting, *Vir Heroicus Sublimis*
(The Museum of Modern Art, New York), into an eighteen-foot-
long knitted blanket (private collection).

Stacy Levy
Seeing the Path of the Wind, 1991
Weathervane, anemometer, indoor weather
station, electric fans, one thousand organza flags,
rubber stoppers, steel rods, and silver compass points
Diameter 40' (12.2 m); height of flags 3' (0.9 m)
Installation at Moore College of Art and Design,
Philadelphia

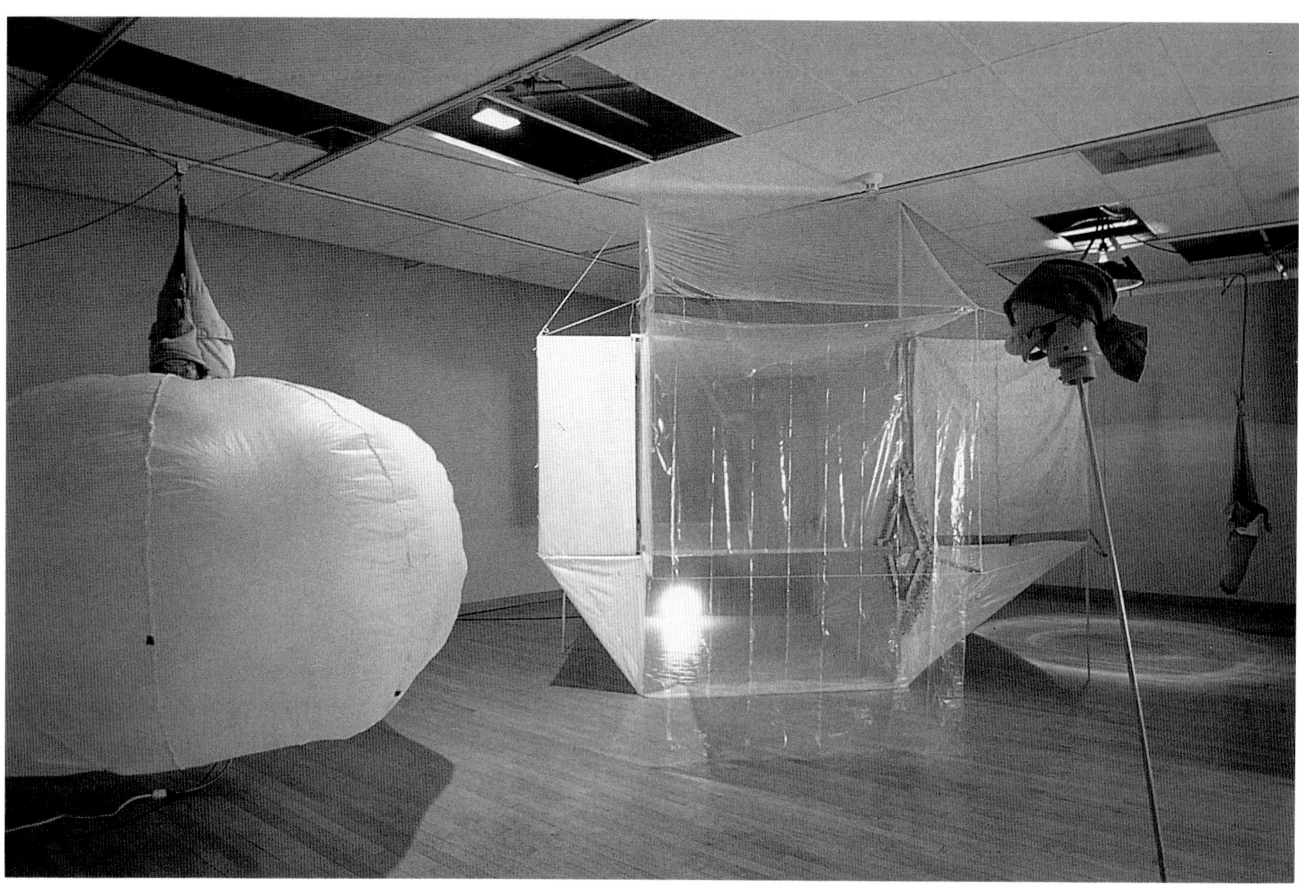

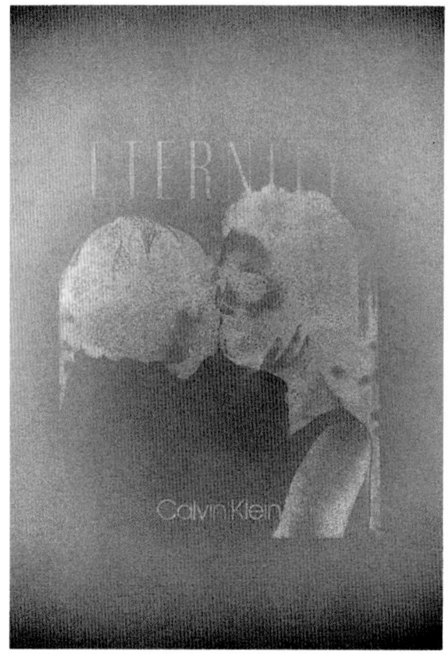

FIGURE 7
Stuart Netsky
Eternity, 1992
Flocked AZT, HIVID, VIDEX, and cornstarch,
silk-screened on board
27¾ × 20" (70.5 × 50.8 cm)
Collection of the artist, courtesy Larry Becker
Contemporary Art, Philadelphia

As these examples suggest, many of the artists in the exhibition use painstaking, elaborate processes to make their work. Stained glass, fiberglass casting, large-scale sculpture made with clay coils, and traditional painting methods with layers of oils and wax—these and others represent a mastery of craft and technique that is a foundation for innovation. In some cases the evidence of time and effort is made so prominent a feature of the work as to take on a symbolic function. Lanny Bergner's sculpture is often formed by many minute, repetitive actions, and the intensity of their cumulative effect places his work on the edge between the overtly handmade and the seemingly self-generated (figure 8). Other artists in the show incorporate the evidence of laborious handwork as an allusion to the passage of time. The process of building up and scraping down surfaces in paintings and drawings by Bruce Pollock, Stephen Talasnik, and Charles Burwell acquires an evolutionary quality, providing potent metaphors for cycles of growth and decay and for archaeological layerings of human culture.

The identity that long characterized the art of the Philadelphia region was founded on representations of the human body, a tradition that reached its height in the late nineteenth century with the figures and portraits of Thomas Eakins, which were grounded in his thorough studies of human anatomy. The body continues to be a central concern among contemporary artists in the area, although its treatment spans an extremely broad range, including classical figurative painting, stylized portraiture, performative self-portrait photography, and semiabstract body surrogates. This persistence of the body as a subject and the variety of approaches to it reflect an ongoing national and international argument between figuration and "body art." Figuration builds on the traditions in many cultures of representing the human form as a central means for conveying ideas and emotions. Body art derives from more recent practices in performance, video, and photography that emphasize the materiality of the body as a physical, psychological, and ideological site, rather than as a form to be represented.

While their approaches to the depiction of the body vary greatly, Lisa Bartolozzi, Frank Galuszka, and Susan Moore all build on the figurative tradition. Bartolozzi's figures and fragments are exquisitely modeled, joining convincing illusion with dramatic presentation. Galuszka's paintings—which have ranged from detailed realism to dazzling abstraction over the past twenty years, sometimes within the same work (figure 9)—center on images of family members, acquaintances, and other models, including mythological figures such as the all-devouring Indian goddess Kali. Both artists embrace narrative and allegorical content, but of a distinctly contemporary type in which the stories and meanings that motivate an image are left open-ended, inviting viewers to form their own interpretations. Like Galuszka and Bartolozzi, Moore works with an intense awareness of what it means to paint the figure in the late twentieth century. With their heavily textured surfaces, unnatural colors, and tight cropping (figure 10), her close-ups of faces, often on a monumental scale, and her figures seen from behind present a fine balance between illusionistic human presence and formalist abstraction.

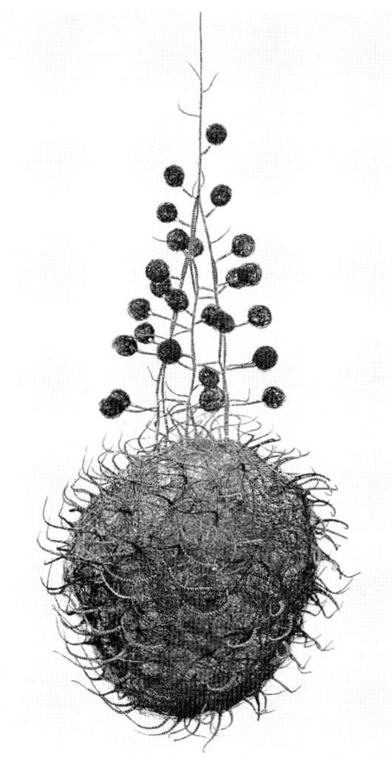

Lanny Bergner
Spin, 1996
Screen and wire
39 × 16" (99.1 × 40.6 cm)
Collection of the artist

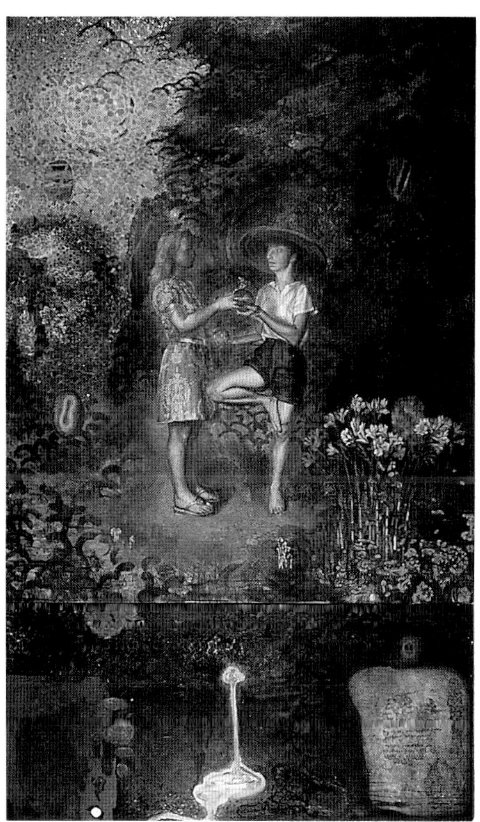

Frank Galuszka
Wissahickon: A Partial View IV, 1995
Oil on linen
84 × 68" (213.4 × 172.7 cm)
Courtesy The More Gallery, Inc.,
Philadelphia

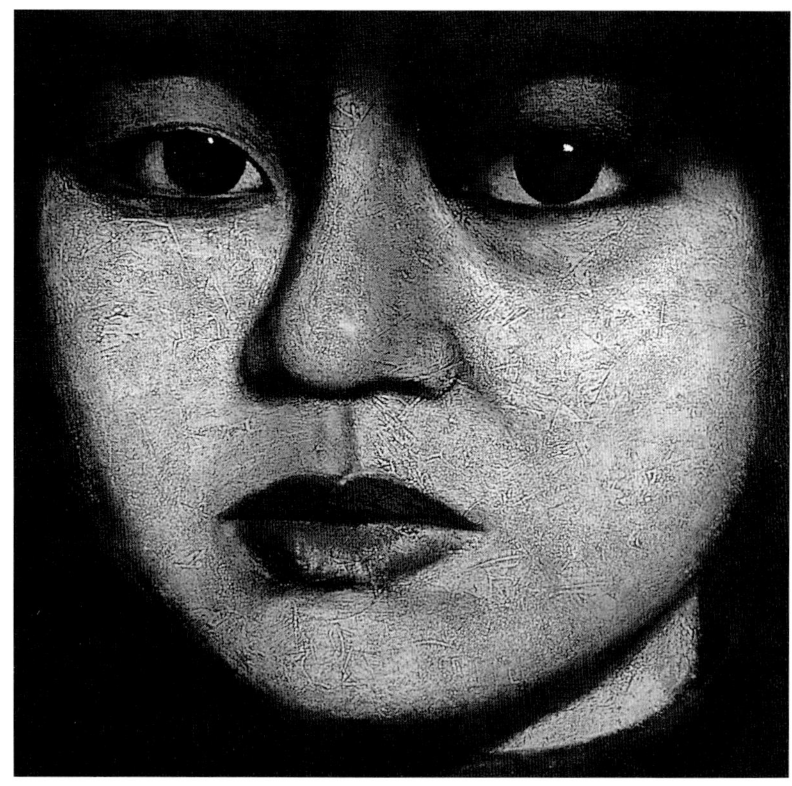

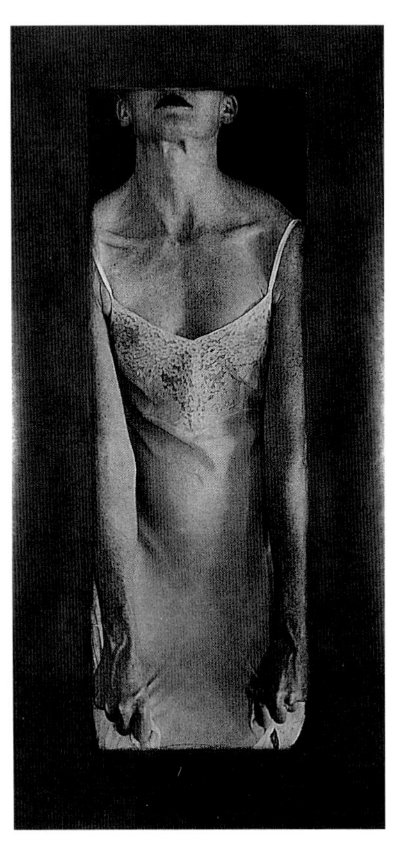

Kate Moran's large-scale photographs of herself, on the other hand, are based in a performative approach, appearing as moments of intense emotion frozen from ongoing dramas (figure 11). Her interest in the body as a site of social and personal conflict extends to making wax dolls, motorized ceramic automatons, and metal sculpture based on clothing, all of which read as psychologically charged surrogates for human presence. Similarly, Gabriel Martinez's photographs are based in performance and an understanding of the body as an ideological battleground (figure 12). His images of the physical imperfections of his own body unite vanity and self-exposure to critique social norms, an approach also taken in his live performance events.

This concern with the human body being subject to degradation or aberration reflects current themes of international art addressed by artists such as Kiki Smith, Robert Gober, and Matthew Barney, who cast the body in a distinctly antiheroic light to comment on dominant value systems. Other artists in the exhibition in addition to Moran and Martinez share this interest in the underside of the human experience. Tristin Lowe chooses as his hero the clown, a figure whose reason for being is to make a fool of himself in public; Brooke Moyer suggests desiccated shells of living beings with his hollow fiberglass and resin sculptures (figure 13); and Stuart Netsky explores the ravages of time and disease on our bodies and our ideals with his sculptures and installations incorporating latex sheeting, AIDS drugs, and casts of eroded classical statuary.

An often-heard question is whether these artistic concerns and strategies run the risk of glorifying rather than critiquing the victimization of the physical and psychological self. However, as many of the artists in this exhibition demonstrate, embracing a marginalized or oppressed perspective can provide a powerful position of resistance against a dominating cultural mainstream. Others in the show are concerned with a more broadly recognized transformative power of art, whereby negative experiences provide the source for powerful expression. In either case, it is an entirely fitting moment, as we near the turning of a millennium—historically a time of heightened moral, social, and spiritual questioning—to face the difficult realities and unresolved dilemmas put forth by the artists whose work we celebrate here.

1. In 1990–91 and 1991–92, Fleisher experimented with five *Challenge* shows per year to accommodate more of the growing pool of applicants, giving fifteen artists the opportunity to exhibit in each of those two years. The increased schedule, however, proved unmanageable and made the exhibitions too short.

2. Donald B. Kuspit, "Sol LeWitt: The Look of Thought," *Art in America*, vol. 63, no. 5 (September–October 1975), pp. 43–49.

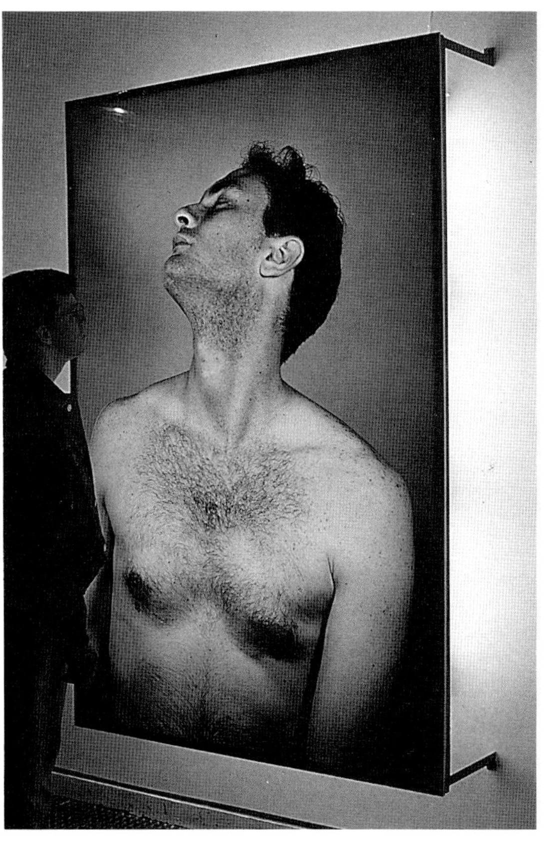

FIGURE 12
Gabriel Martinez
Anterior Torso and Facial Features, 1994
Duratrans display material in light box
72 × 48 × 12" (182.9 × 121.9 × 30.5 cm)
Collection of the artist

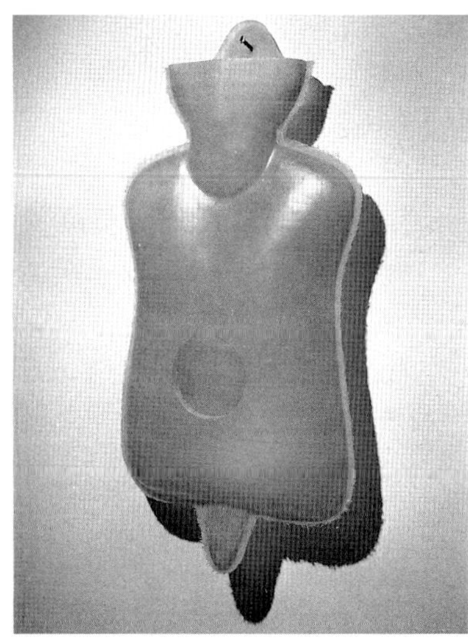

FIGURE 13
Brooke Moyer
Exovoid, 1997
Epoxy resin and fiberglass
37 × 19 × 6" (94 × 48.3 × 15.2 cm)
Collection of the artist

THORA JACOBSON

The city is essentially a meeting place. It is valued by the character of its availabilities. Our way of life is born of freedom which has inspired availabilities the like of which no nation has. The character of this freedom is so great that even a law must adjust to its unmeasurable qualities.

When I was in my early teens, I went to the Graphic Sketch Club. I walked from 7th and Poplar to 8th and Catherine [sic]. I was given an easel, paper and charcoal in the life class. All I could hear was the swishing of the strokes and the soft and privately directed voice of the critic. It was a meeting availability, a place full of offerings.[1]

In December 1973, less than four months before his death, the architect Louis I. Kahn wrote the above testimonial for his first art school, the Graphic Sketch Club, which later was renamed the Samuel S. Fleisher Art Memorial.[2] In writing about this "place full of offerings," Kahn was paying homage to an extraordinary institution that helped to give form to a young boy's dreams and aspirations (see figure 14).

By the mid-1970s, when Kahn was looking back on his experience at Fleisher, artists in Philadelphia had been mobilizing for some time around the issues they considered basic to survival: how to have their work exhibited, reviewed, and collected. Fleisher, with its long history as "a meeting availability" for the region's artists, seemed to be ideally poised to make an important contribution toward the realization of these goals. The creation of the

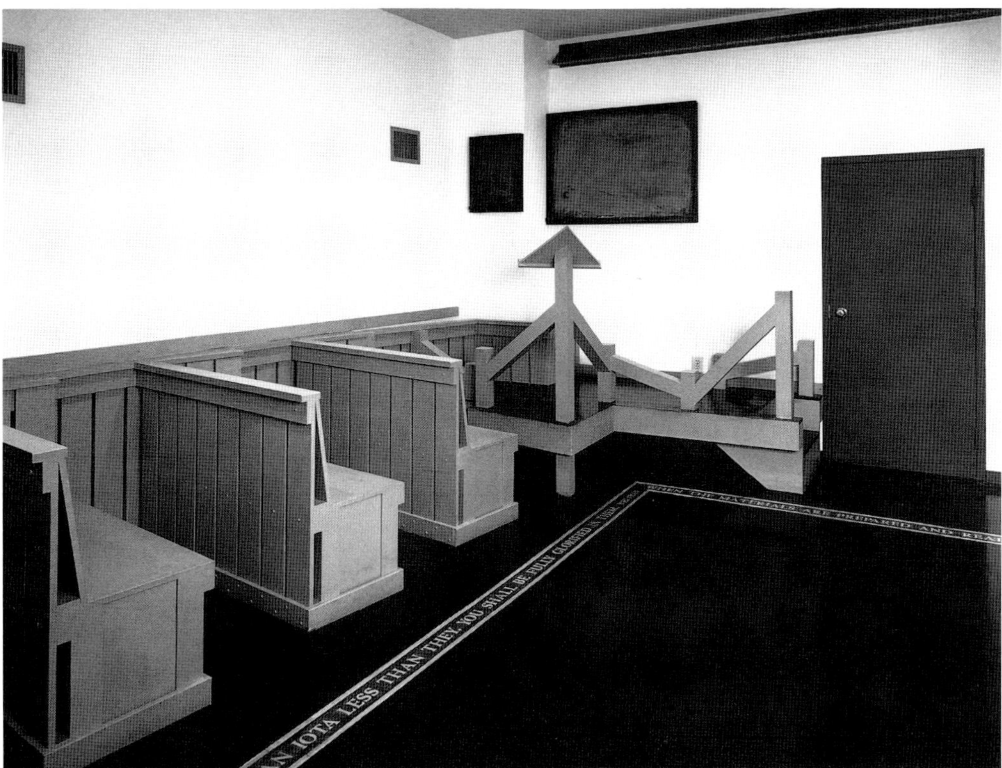

Challenge exhibitions at the Art Memorial in 1977–78, as an institutional commitment and inclusive call to working artists living within a fifty-mile radius of Philadelphia, helped to foster a tentative, if fragmentary, sense that Philadelphia was indeed a good place for artists to live and work.

While they had reason for optimism, area artists of the 1970s had also experienced a long period of disappointment. The list of exhibition venues was distressingly short, especially considering the quantity and quality of the art schools in Philadelphia, and the physical limitations, location, and management of many further diminished their appeal. Moreover, points of access— whether through juried or invitational group shows or solo exhibitions—were often either invisible to or jealously guarded from local artists. Racism, sexism, and the hegemony of the figurative tradition in local schools and commercial galleries had further narrowed the frame of reference.

Many artists did not have commercial representation, which was not surprising given the fact that in the late 1970s the area's galleries could be counted on less than two hands. However, the few that did exist, including the Marian Locks, Janet Fleisher, Langman, Mangel, Gross McCleaf, and Works galleries, were nurturing a reputation for showing local and national artists and craftspersons in a variety of mediums.

The Louis Kahn Lecture Room at the Samuel S. Fleisher Art Memorial, designed by Siah Armajani, was commissioned by the Fairmount Park Art Association in 1982. The northern cornice of the room is inscribed with a quote from Kahn: "The school is a realm of spaces where it is good to learn."

Beyond the commercial galleries, exhibition possibilities were at best fragmented, and the opportunities for inclusion in major public collections were few. Except for the Cheltenham Center for the Arts' long-standing juried painting exhibition that offered the coveted Philadelphia Museum of Art purchase prize, the Print Club's annual juried show that presented award-winning prints and photographs to the Philadelphia Museum of Art, and the Pennsylvania Academy of the Fine Arts Fellowship annual, there were only limited avenues through which the work of regional artists could enter the holdings of major area institutions.

Still, the establishment of the Fleisher *Challenge* series in the late 1970s was not the only sign of promise for the Philadelphia arts community of the time. The creation of *Challenge* came on the heels of the founding of Nexus as the city's first artist-run space and network in 1976. Then, in 1978, the Pennsylvania Academy launched the Morris Gallery program of solo exhibitions of artists with Philadelphia—but not just Academy—affiliations. Elsewhere in 1978, the Institute of Contemporary Art at the University of Pennsylvania already had an impressive history of bringing nationally known contemporary artists to the city, although it offered an admittedly less convincing track record of showing the work of area artists. Also during this period, Helen Drutt, whose advocacy for crafts—local, national, and international—remains unparalleled to this day, was organizing exhibitions in the galleries at Moore College of Art and Design. It was during her tenure at Moore as well that Drutt and Harry Anderson began the energizing series of *Opens Friday* exhibitions at the college. In the midst of all of these variously successful attempts at expanding the exhibition opportunities for artists, the Philadelphia Art Alliance serenely maintained its venerable role as the principal noncommercial gallery in center-city Philadelphia.

Exacerbating the paucity of exhibition possibilities was the impoverished state of the local art press. Even reviews in the city's major dailies suffered from lack of space and were often, of necessity, more informational than critical in nature. National coverage was limited to only two or three shows a year, usually those at the major institutions. While glimmers of hope came locally with the founding of *Arts Exchange* and the *New Art*

Examiner, which did much to raise the level of criticism, they were not widely read beyond the ranks of the converted.

Within such an atmosphere in dire need of improvement, Fleisher occupied an especially advantageous position by virtue of its many years as an arts educator, employer, exhibition venue, collector, and advocate (see figure 15). Although the lion's share of Fleisher's art collections had gone into storage in 1974, it had acquired a sizable body of work largely by Philadelphia artists at the Association of American Artists shows in the 1960s. A complex history of Philadelphia and American art was also literally embedded in its walls, windows, and doorways. Along the western wall of the Fleisher Sanctuary, for example, stretches a series of murals by a young Robert Henri, a leading figure in the Modernist movement in Philadelphia and beyond; other murals at Fleisher are the work of Nicola D'Ascenzo, who would later be known for his distinguished stained-glass programs for public buildings, and the iron gate of the Sanctuary was commissioned

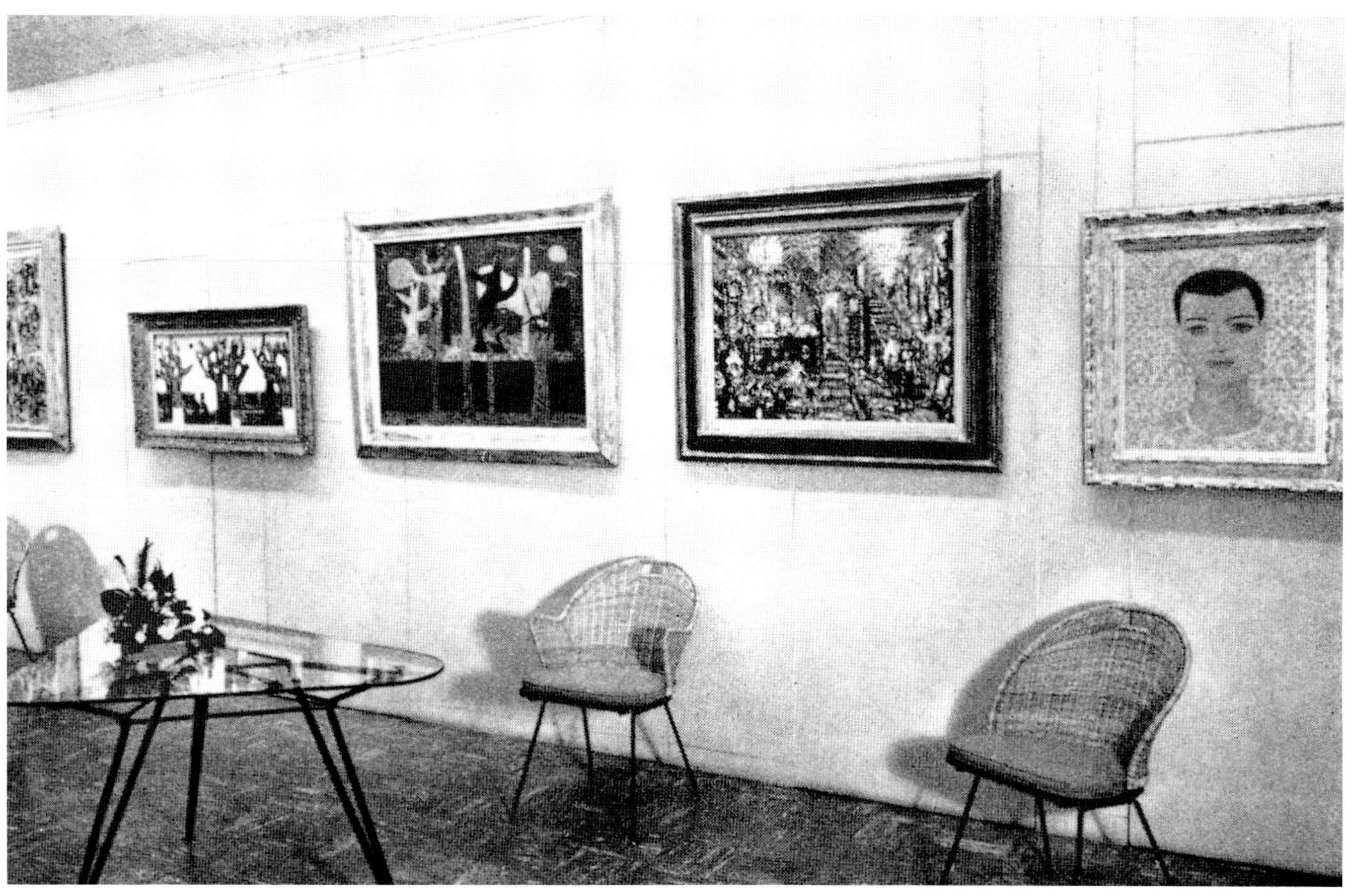

FIGURE 15

The Gallery for Contemporary Art at the Fleisher Art Memorial, c. 1959, with work by regional artists from the Memorial's permanent collection (from Irene N. Zieget, *History of the Samuel S. Fleisher Art Memorial: The Sanctuary, The Art School, 1886–1963* [Philadelphia, 1963], repro. p. 28)

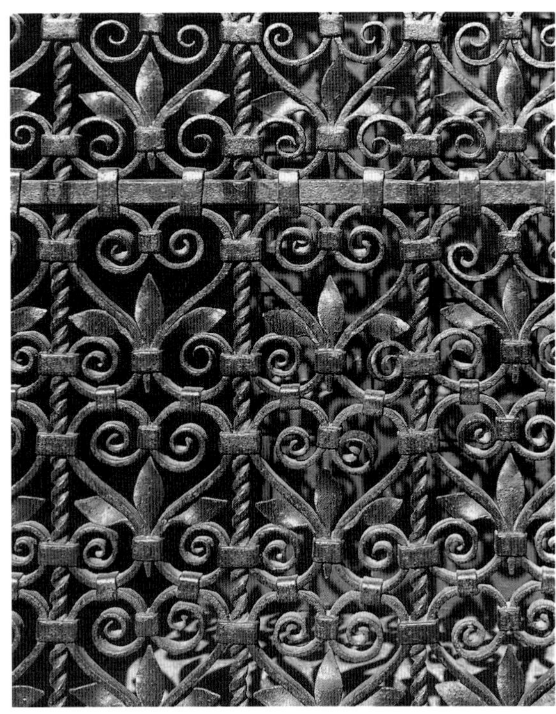

Detail of the iron gate of the Sanctuary at the Fleisher Art
Memorial, commissioned by Samuel Fleisher from
Philadelphia artisan Samuel Yellin in 1935

in 1935 from the noted Philadelphia craftsman Samuel Yellin
(figure 16).

In deciding to establish the *Challenge* series, Fleisher could
also draw on the rich experience it had gained from the wide
range of exhibitions it had sponsored in the previous decade: a
large, commemorative group show to mark the Memorial's sev-
entieth anniversary in 1968; a teaching exhibition on shape,
form, and color organized by artist and educator Penny Balkin
Bach and her students from the Parkway Program (Philadelphia's
"high school without walls") in 1971; a retrospective of the work
of local artist and Fleisher alumnus Sam Maitin in 1972; *In Her
Own Image,* a major exhibition of the work of women artists, in
1974; and the community-based *Rites of Passage* exhibitions that
included artifacts and photographs from several of Philadelphia's
major ethnic groups in 1975 and 1976. Despite such successes,
however, Fleisher's relatively modest schedule of exhibitions was
still built firmly around the in-house shows of the work of students and faculty, whose selection was guided less by policy than
by serendipity and a complicated sense of tradition.

While Fleisher's revered position in the Philadelphia visual
arts community ultimately did play an undeniably major role in
informing the creation and structure of *Challenge,* the prospect of
such a regular exhibitions program that limited future choices
and required additional resources was not immediately popular
with the Memorial's governing board and staff.

But in framing the nature of the *Challenge* series, Fleisher
found that it could rely on the currency of goodwill that had
accumulated during its more than eighty years of direct relationships with artists. From the outset, artists have been at the heart
of the *Challenge* exhibitions—as the constituency served, the primary audience, and the decision-makers who would, over the
next twenty years, guide its evolving program and focus. In developing the program Fleisher rejected the notion of sponsoring yet
another regional juried show, having neither the storage space nor
the personnel to make such a venture feasible. Additionally, the
decision was made to allow participating artists to show a more
complete body of work than traditional juried shows allow.

The first year of the *Challenge* exhibitions, 1978–79, yielded a modest field of seventy applicants. It is a tribute to the quality of the artists who submitted slides, the wisdom of the artists who served as the first jurors, and the impact of early and regular reviews written by Victoria Donohoe of the *Inquirer* and Nessa Forman of the *Bulletin* that the credibility of the series was established. Within a year, the number of applicants had grown to almost two hundred. At this stage Fleisher then called on its second greatest asset—its historical relationship with the Philadelphia Museum of Art—for guidance. It was agreed that the competition had grown to the point that it needed a two-staged selection process, which the Museum's curators enthusiastically joined as a useful way of supporting the *Challenge* series while broadening their own knowledge of the community and their awareness of individual artists' growth. The decision to hire a working artist to manage the program after its second year also proved invaluable, for these people have brought to the series an attentiveness to artists' concerns as well as a commitment to enhancing both the reach and quality of the exhibitions.

Throughout its twenty-year history, the *Challenge* chronicle has developed in the context of an arts community that has changed both internally and externally (see figure 17). Fleisher itself underwent a change in structure and leadership, as several of its long time faculty either died or retired and were replaced by younger instructors who worked with new mediums, disciplines, and notions about art. The meaning of *"Challenge"* itself also took on a new dimension, for the work in the exhibitions often differed dramatically from the activities and perspectives of Fleisher's students and faculty.

In 1983, in recognition of the need for the Memorial to seek funds independently, a distinct not-for-profit corporation with its own board of directors and identity was established, a move that would have profound implications on Fleisher's self perception and its motivation to develop its programs and facilities. The implementation of this decision coincided roughly with the fifth anniversary of the *Challenge* program and a reunion of the sixty artists who had shown at Fleisher from 1978 to 1983. Hosted at the Philadelphia Art Alliance from November 5 to December 10, 1983, this exhibition, which attracted more than

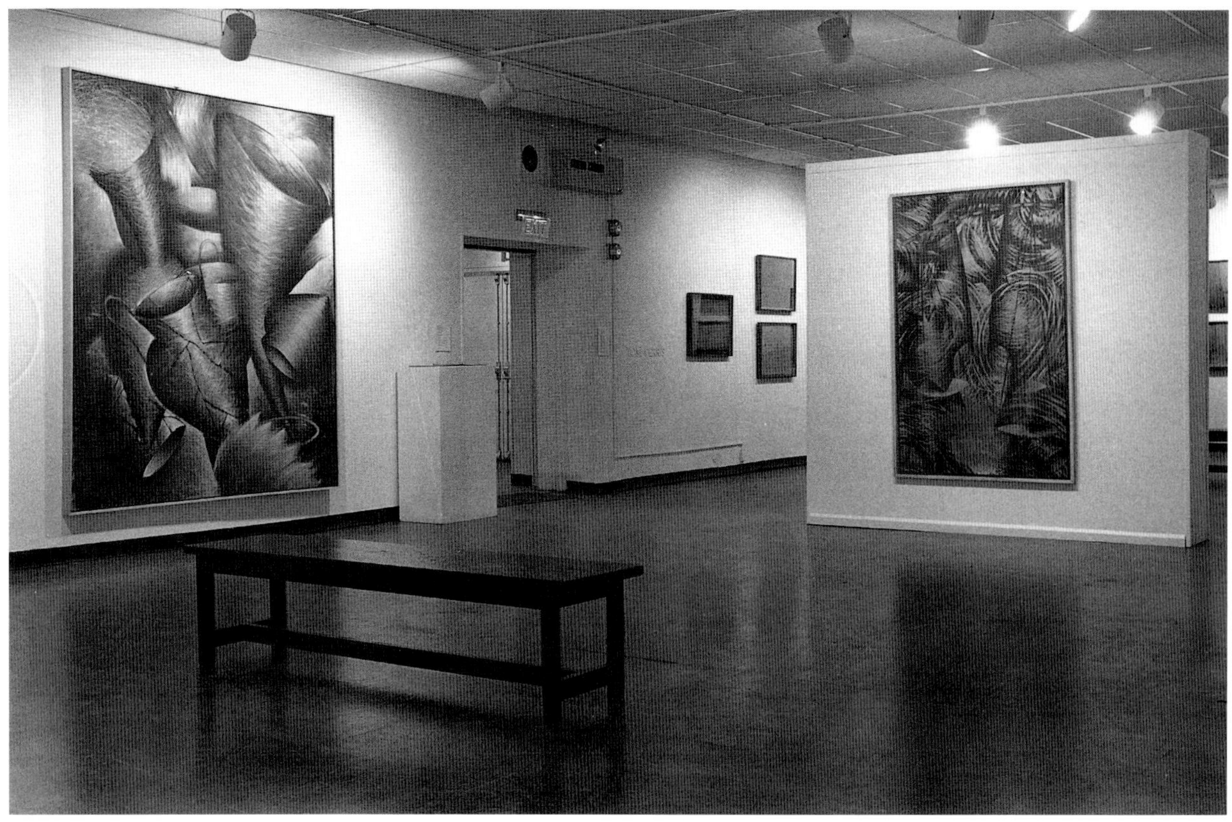

six hundred people to the opening reception, confirmed both the vitality of the arts community it served and the value of the *Challenge* experience to the participating artists and to Fleisher itself.

By this time, a number of the artists who had been selected for *Challenge* in its first five years had received fellowships from the Pennsylvania Council on the Arts, the National Endowment for the Arts, and the American Academy in Rome. Many also had developed gallery affiliations, and some had been selected for solo exhibitions at the region's major institutions. Several artists in this group found their first devoted collectors and received their first national reviews as a result of *Challenge*.

Outside Fleisher, the decade of the 1980s brought an era of mixed messages for Philadelphia-area artists. On the positive side, leading institutions were developing multiple strategies for exhibiting and acquiring works of art by regional artists. *Pertaining to Philadelphia,* an intermittent exhibition and program strategy at the Philadelphia Museum of Art, along with the creation of the Julius Bloch Memorial Fund for the acquisition of works of art by Philadelphia-area artists, opened new, dual avenues of support for local artists at the Museum. *Made in Philadelphia,* an ongoing series of group shows at the Institute of Contemporary Art, provided thematic perspectives on the region's expanding pluralism. And the Morris Gallery program at the Pennsylvania

Academy of the Fine Arts extended its commitment by jealously guarding the main first-floor exhibition space for artists with links to Philadelphia.

During the 1980s new commercial galleries were also beginning to pop up along Walnut Street in Philadelphia, and several corporations and law firms started to fill their walls with the work of area artists, with some even establishing regular exhibition programs to showcase local art. Many of these opportunities became predictable venues, although they were available only to artists whose work was appropriate for a corporate environment.

Noncommercial venues started to emerge in response to this growth in commercial activity. Upon assuming the position of director of the galleries at Moore College of Art, Elsa Longhauser recognized the need to attract audiences other than students. She also realized that those audiences had to see the work of artists who had achieved national and international prominence as well as the many area artists who had received neither critical attention nor interpretation. This led to the creation of the Levy Gallery for the Arts in Philadelphia at Moore, which, under the direction of Richard Torchia, explored Philadelphia's artistic *terra incognita*, unearthing artists who dealt with a range of unfamiliar art forms and subjects.

The years of Mayor Wilson Goode's administration (1984–92) brought about the inauguration of the *Art in City Hall* series, which reinforced the revolution of rising expectations among artists. The 1980s also signaled important new opportunities for sculptors through the revitalization and growth of public art programs. With both the revival (although somewhat halting) of the city's Percent for Art Program and the expansion of the number of names considered for commissions from the Redevelopment Authority, Philadelphia artists actually began to seek and find work in parks and public buildings. The founding of the Clay Studio, the emergence of new cooperative galleries such as Vox Populi and Muse, the development of the gallery program and the New Forms projects by the Painted Bride, and the myriad ambitions of an ever-lengthening list of other community art centers all served to make Philadelphia an increasingly attractive environment for working artists in the 1980s.

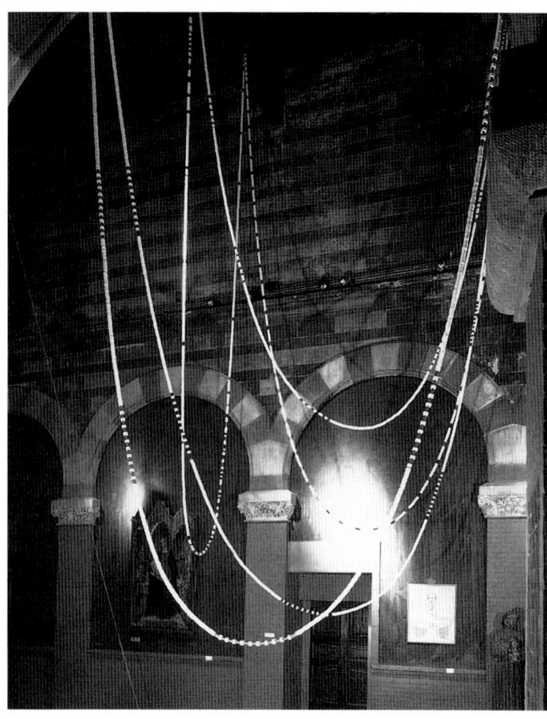

Richard Jordan's *Cosmic Mass (Dedicated to John Coltrane),* constructed of Bianco Macedonian marble and fabric, was one of seven site-specific installations created for *10 × 12,* an exhibition that celebrated the tenth anniversary of *Challenge* in September–October 1988

At the same time, however, during the last half of the decade the relationship between artists and audiences all over the United States came to be redefined under the imprecise but volatile term "culture wars." Whether their work was difficult because of provocative imagery or hermetic language, political opinion or personal indignation, artists found this period to be marked by a critical disconnection between themselves and their public. Philadelphia, like other places in the country, felt repercussions from the controversy over an exhibition of Robert Mapplethorpe photographs, which had earlier been shown at the Institute of Contemporary Art, and other skirmishes occurred when two *Art in City Hall* exhibitions met with censorship over politically sensitive issues.

These situations were symptomatic of a widening gap between the goals of artists, including many of those in Philadelphia, and the perceptions of the communities in which they worked. At Fleisher, it led to the creation of the *TalkAbout* as part of the *Challenge* series in 1986. A regular, facilitated dialogue led by an artist/critic during evening classes, *TalkAbout* has become one of the Memorial's most vital educational tools over the past twelve years. It is frequently attended by the exhibiting *Challenge* artists, and consistently brings both artists and student audiences together to test their assumptions, broaden their collective visual experience, and encourage informed critical responses.

In 1988 the apparent chasm between local artists and audiences led to the *City of the Imagination,* Philadelphia's first two-day gathering of artists, administrators, funders, *and* framers of cultural policy. This meeting, for which Fleisher acted as co-sponsor and host, shifted the focus of discourse from an abstract notion of art-that-provokes to one that examines how artists function in society, and thereby subtly but effectively galvanized the region's artists into activists. Over time their agitation through the Arts Emergency Coalition, which grew out of this conference, has served to pry open some institutional doors while propping others open long enough to have a discernible impact on institutional policy.

City of the Imagination also coincided with the tenth anniversary of the *Challenge* exhibitions, a moment that tested the impact of the series, and drew the school and gallery closer together. In searching out a venue for that anniversary exhibition, Gallery Coordinator Lanny Bergner recommended that Fleisher in its entirety offer both the space (37,000 square feet) and the "sense of place" that would allow for formal as well as informal settings for installations.

Of the original group of 120 Fleisher *Challenge* artists, 110 responded to the invitation to participate in *10 × 12,* with seven creating site-specific installations at the Memorial (see figure 18). Using the galleries, Sanctuary, stairwells, and studios, the exhibition was, on one hand, a confrontation between artists and audiences and, on the other, a *rapprochement.* By means of *10 × 12,* which enlivened classroom discussion at Fleisher for months and attracted a record number of applications for *Challenge* in the following year, Fleisher had reconnected with its roots in arts education and rejuvenated its perspective.

A new spirit of activism was similarly felt, directly and indirectly, with both the Philadelphia Art Now juried exhibition, *Contemporary Philadelphia Artists,* held at the Philadelphia Museum of Art in 1990, and the response of the artists' community, *Art at the Armory,* shown at the same time. Since then, this energy has been felt in the creation and evolution of the selection process for the Pew Fellowships in the Arts, in the impressive inclusion of regional artists' work at the new Pennsylvania Convention Center in Philadelphia, and in the ways that all art organizations in the Philadelphia area—including Fleisher— reach their audiences, make curatorial selections, and respond to "challenges" innovatively.

Arranged Introductions, a program established by Mary Griffin and Carlota Schoolman at Fleisher in 1992–93, has further served to invigorate programming, linking the Memorial both with its community institutions and with artists working thoughtfully in interdisciplinary ways and new settings (see figure 19). Among the artists who have been brought to Fleisher under the program's residency project are Elizabeth Streb, who worked with a Vietnamese Boy Scout troop in a local settlement house; Diamanda Galas, who used Fleisher itself as context and inspiration for a memorial to her late brother; Homer Jackson,

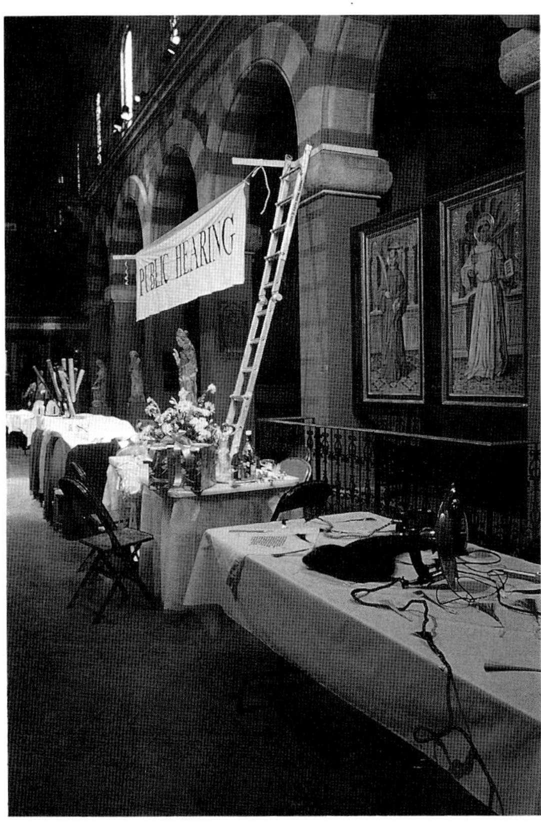

FIGURE 19

Historias/Public Hearing, an installation and performance by Pepon Osorio and Merian Soto that examined the complex dynamics of Puerto Rican and "Nuyorican" cultures, was part of the *Arranged Introductions* program in the Fleisher Sanctuary in January 1992

who developed projects with the staff at the Franklin Institute; and Jonas Dos Santos, who collaborated with Fleisher staff and neighborhood children to create a multimedia exhibition and performance. With each experience, it became increasingly clear that relationships between artist and audience are rarely forged in a single transformative moment, but rather are most effective when they are revealed slowly, over time, considered by both creator and viewer throughout the process, and understood within a context of community that is mutable as well as comprehensible.

Among the most important changes in the Philadelphia arts community over the past twenty years has been a globalization of perspective. Despite Fleisher's regional emphasis, it too has grasped the need to recontextualize the work it exhibits in light of art being created elsewhere. In 1990, for example, Fleisher worked with Spanish-born artist Miralda on a project that linked two local traditional art forms in a major international performance piece involving thirty-five mummers' clubs, the Fabric Workshop, and the Philadelphia Museum of Art. And, more recently, in collaboration with the Institute of Contemporary Art, Fleisher invited Irish artist John Kindness for a month-long residency that was then folded into a major retrospective at the ICA.

As major institutions in the region, including Fleisher, have taken seriously the importance of showing the work produced in this area, they have also found it increasingly important to show how that work is viewed and valued in an ever wider and more complex context. It is this responsive process that, at the distance

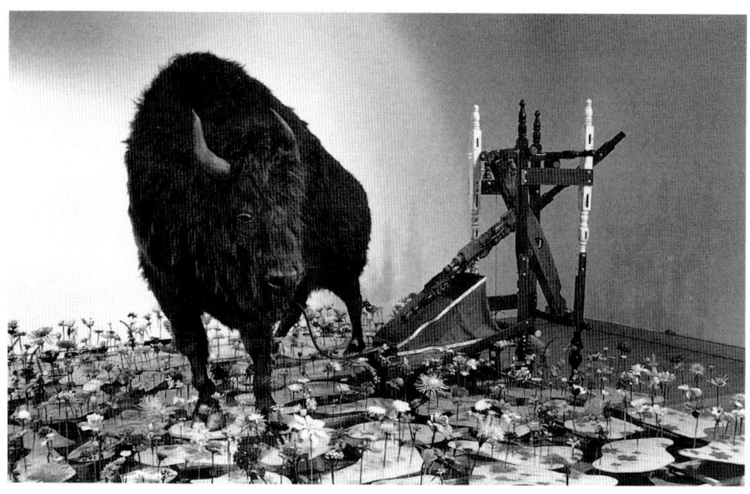

FIGURE 20
Hilary Harp's *Resuscitated Bison: Field of Flowers* was installed in the *Challenge* exhibition of November–December 1994

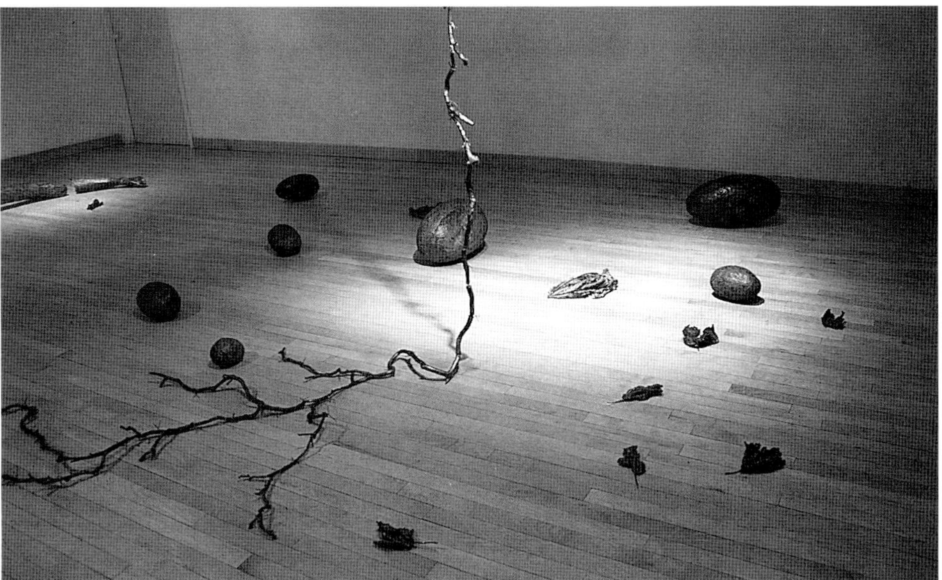

of twenty years, has served so well both the *Challenge* exhibitions, with their flexible, artist-centered and -directed format, and the enriched local arts environment (see figures 20, 21). *Challenge* has secured its role in Fleisher's programming while at the same time signaling the commitment of the institution to artists at all stages in their careers and in all of their various roles, as the panoply of local opportunities has expanded to reflect a widening range of subject, discipline, function, and cultural diversity.

This exhibition at the Philadelphia Museum of Art includes 20 of the 248 artists who have shown as part of *Challenge* over the past twenty years. It is but one manifestation of the efforts of an impressive and increasingly cohesive community of skilled and imaginative artists, institutions, and audiences who have learned to value each other for their contributions—individual and collective—and who share in the complex sense of optimism that abounds in 1998. Fleisher and its partners in the support of regional artists have, since 1978, all contributed to a new generation of "usual suspects." It is the increasing pluralism of the Philadelphia area's creative output, as well as the diversity of the artists making it and audiences viewing it, that compels all art institutions to accept a far more complex challenge than existed twenty years ago. We are obliged to keep our doors, eyes, and minds open to a wider understanding of what constitutes art. At the Samuel S. Fleisher Art Memorial, we work to meet this external challenge at the same time as we treasure Louis Kahn's view of our institution as "a place full of offerings."

1. Quoted in *Philadelphia Museum of Art Bulletin,* vol. 68, no. 309 (Spring 1974), p. 56.
2. Founded by Samuel S. Fleisher in 1898 as the Graphic Sketch Club, the name was changed to the Samuel S. Fleisher Art Memorial in 1945 under the terms of Fleisher's will.

FIGURE 21
The January–February 1998 *Challenge* exhibition included Cynthia Porter's installation *Deep Dreaming*

Lisa Bartolozzi	Gabriel Martinez
Lanny Bergner	Susan Moore
Norinne Betjemann	Kate Moran
Charles Burwell	Brooke Moyer
Syd Carpenter	Don Nakamura
Frank Galuszka	Stuart Netsky
Michael Grothusen	Bruce Pollock
Mei-ling Hom	Judith Schaechter
Stacy Levy	Hester Stinnett
Tristin Lowe	Stephen Talasnik

Lisa Bartolozzi

Throughout her career Lisa Bartolozzi's one constant subject has been the human figure, most often nude, painted both full-length and partially, and sometimes as mere fragments isolated against a dark ground. Her works have an intensity that combines the detailed realism of the Northern Renaissance with the dramatic compositions and lighting of the Italian Baroque. She achieves the effect of figures palpably modeled in space by using traditional glazing techniques, building her image slowly with layers of transparent and semitransparent oil pigments interspersed with coats of wax buffed with cloths and her bare hands.

The human figure, according to Bartolozzi, is the "most direct vehicle for expressing universal concepts about humankind,"[1] with the immediacy of the realistically painted nude having the power to evoke empathy and to engage viewers in the drama of the image. Bartolozzi keeps the symbolism of her figures simple. She wants them to function on an archetypal level, although she is not interested in making images of a generalized ideal. She prefers instead to render the sagging flesh, wrinkled brows, and crooked smiles that make the figures real. Her attention to detail also gives her figures their contemporaneity—even as nudes, their expressions, body types, and poses distinguish them from their historical counterparts.

Bartolozzi often uses unusually shaped canvases or sculptural frames that set her images deeply back in a boxlike space or thrust them forward. She has also mounted paintings on two-sided freestanding panels that enhance their presence as independent objects in space while recalling the tradition of church altarpieces. In *Tell Us About Magdelene* (checklist 1), for example, the female figure seems to rest on the narrow shelf at the bottom, thereby bridging the gap not only between pictorial and real space but between past and present time, as she seems ready to offer a live account of a historical event.

The themes of Bartolozzi's paintings are drawn from issues that she is addressing in her own life, for as she describes, "I don't paint a figure if I haven't gone through what I think I'm putting my women and men through."[2] She painted *Model* (plate 1) in part as a meditation on the question of her place as a woman and a painter in relation to the tradition of the nude. The image is grounded in an exquisitely detailed rendering of an individual—a young man who appears in a number of her earlier pieces—but Bartolozzi balances the sense of a unique personality with the notion of the model as a blank canvas on which to express her own feelings and thoughts about the relationship between the artist and her hired sitter. She has made his expression simultaneously self-knowing and unformed, and placed the image in a frame that projects its subject forward as we project onto him.

Although she often begins her paintings with a personal story as motivation, Bartolozzi, like many contemporary artists working with narrative and allegory, is happy to leave the finished work open to multiple interpretations. Bartolozzi signals the symbolic intent of her images by their distilled intensity, the way in which every aspect of the work, from surface treatment to pose and gesture, conveys a sense of invested meanings. Even when inspired by textual sources such as the Bible, she strives for a balance between specificity and open-endedness. Her *Marking of Foreheads* (checklist 2), for example, is inspired by Albrecht Dürer's woodcut based on the account in the Apocalypse of how a mark is placed on the forehead of those who are going to be saved. The front of this freestanding painting shows a man's bald and wrinkled forehead, just enough, the artist has said, to establish the idea of a person.[3] On the reverse, a series of marks scratched into a beeswax panel over a faint image of hands convey the theme of marking suggested in the title and also seem to keep score. It is an image at once literal and enigmatic, interweaving themes of salvation, rationality, and self-evaluation.

1. Artist's talk at Delaware Art Museum, Wilmington, July 10, 1997.
2. Quoted in Delaware Art Museum, Wilmington, *Lisa Bartolozzi: New Paintings and Drawings* (July 11–September 7, 1997), n.p.
3. Conversation with the author, April 24, 1997.

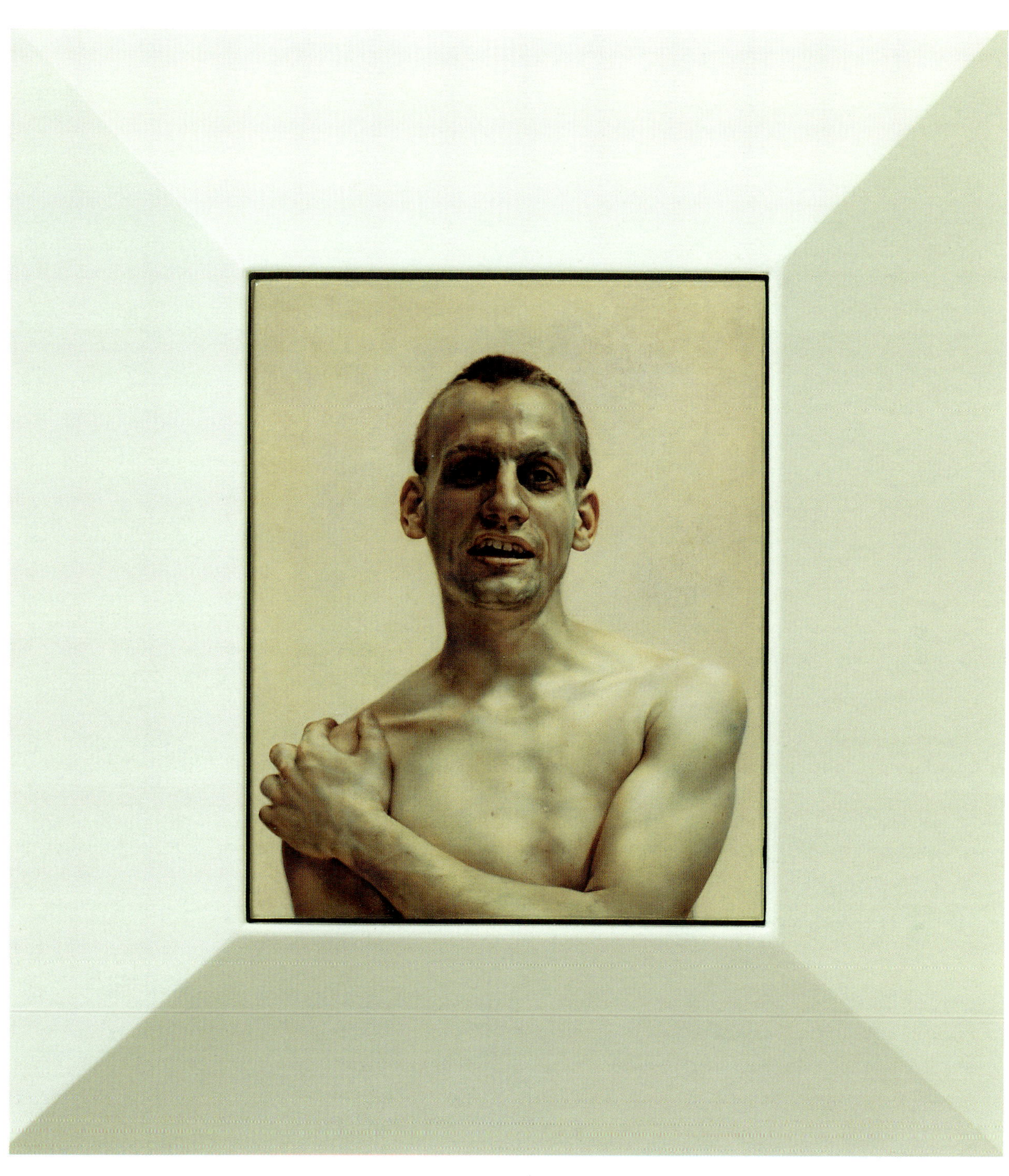

Lisa Bartolozzi
Model, 1997
Oil on panel
10 × 8" (25.4 × 20.3 cm) image
Collection of Mr. and Mrs. E. Hatchadoorian

Lanny Bergner

Lanny Bergner makes unexpectedly beautiful sculptures out of common, nonart materials. These may be functional items from the hardware store (aluminum screening, copper wire, and silicone caulking), the tackle shop (monofilament and fishhooks), or the five-and-dime (nylon stockings and safety pins), or cast-off industrial waste such as slag from abandoned railroad beds. It is in the combination of these humble products, used mainly in their natural states, and in the processes he employs that the transformations occur, revealing a wealth of aesthetic possibilities beyond all expectations raised by their origins.

Bergner has developed various labor-intensive working methods that owe as much to the realm of everyday tasks as to the craft traditions of basketry and weaving. Separating, twisting, splicing, knotting, hooking, and wrapping are common features of his process, particularly in his open hanging pieces. Solid sculptures in slag, silicone, wood, and hydrocal involve similarly detailed, repetitive methods of construction such as setting stones and polishing surfaces. His process-oriented approach has an often noted affinity with so-called women's work; this places him within a growing trend of male artists embracing distinctly non-"male" methods for making sculpture.

Despite the intensive quality of having been made by hand, Bergner's sculptures retain a sense of having generated themselves. At the time of his Fleisher show in 1984, Bergner explained: "My inspiration is derived from complex but visually simple organic forms. I sculpturally respond to these forms by developing systems of construction which in combination with intuitive decisions result in sculptures that appear to have grown into existence."[1] Bergner's pieces most often seem to have an unnameable familiarity with the plant and animal worlds that suggests amalgams of flowers, tubers, insects, primitive underwater life forms, and the dwellings and casings made by various creatures.

His silicone and slag pieces from the early 1990s seem strange hybrids of animal trophies and ancient sculptural fragments. Highly burnished sculptures in black or white from this same period resemble inanimate forms, especially sea-smoothed beach stones.[2] Bergner's most recent work returns to the shifting play between inside and outside, surface and form, of his early work from the mid-1980s as he again but more elaborately explores vessel, cocoon, and shed-skin forms, at times with strong contrasts of black and copper wire (see plate 2).

All Bergner's work, whether solid or open, animate or inanimate in its associations, creates tension between seduction and repulsion. Sparkling, jewellike points of light turn out to be hooks and pins embedded in sticky substances. Glistening surfaces have, on closer inspection, a gelatinous translucency resembling wavy cilia somewhere inside the body. This capacity to both attract and repel—along with the inventive use of materials, meticulous process of making, and imaginative forms—gives Bergner's work its unforgettable impact.

1. Artist's statement, Samuel S. Fleisher Art Memorial, Philadelphia, September 21, 1984.
2. In conversation with the author, Bergner mentioned that he traveled back to his native Washington State to gather pebbles from the beach as models (October 30, 1997). The sculptures were displayed on the floor in clusters, filling the gallery so visitors had the experience of walking among them as along the coast.

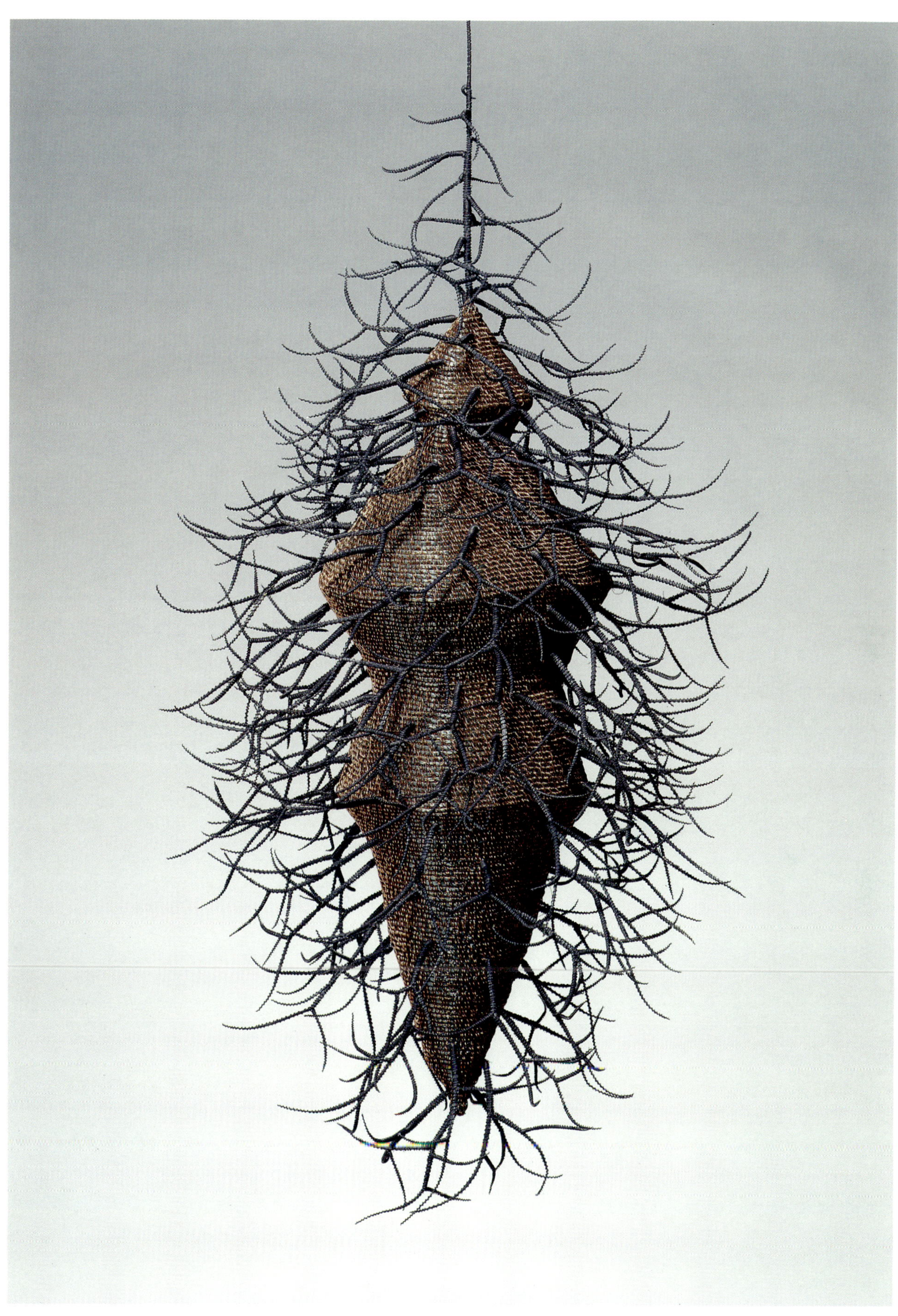

Lanny Bergner
Being Forest, 1997
Screen, monofilament, and copper wire
35 × 15 × 15" (88.9 × 38.1 × 38.1 cm)
Collection of the artist

Norinne Betjemann

Time is a central theme in Norinne Betjemann's work.
She describes wanting to "pierce the membrane of time,"[1]
to create works about the parallel existence of different
periods, and she has developed an elaborate method of
manipulated photography to achieve this goal. Betjemann
travels extensively and shoots slides of the architecture
and, more recently, the landscape of such places as Turkey,
Guatemala, Egypt, the American Southwest, and France.
Her images include well-known sites such as Versailles
and the Hagia Sophia, more local places like Eastern State
Penitentiary in Philadelphia and the National Aquarium
in Baltimore, and many unidentified locations.

In the studio, Betjemann makes large-scale negatives
from her slides, which she considers raw materials to be
cut and combined freely with other images. She sometimes further alters the negatives by scraping or laying on
transparent films, and then prints these spliced negatives
as single images, leaving visible her cut marks and taping
seams. During the developing process, Betjemann splashes
and brushes on the photochemicals to achieve a painterly
quality that keeps the edges fluid and reveals the image
unevenly. She then tints the print with tonal glazes, further painting selected areas with photo oils and gold leaf.

Betjemann's freedom with the conventional boundaries
of photography builds upon the multimedia experiments
of her recent predecessors, notably the Starn Twins, whose
photography-based works from the 1980s often took on
sculptural forms. In the early 1990s, Betjemann experimented with encasing her photographs in thick crusts of
tinted resin to remove them further from the flatness
and fragility of the photographic print. In her most
recent work, she collages and paints on numerous small
photographs—each a fragment of multiple larger
images—that are mounted onto unstretched canvases,
thereby taking photography a step closer to painting.

By manipulating the medium, Betjemann calls attention to the photographic object itself, to the shape of its
edges and the quality of its surface, and so to the image as
a constructed fiction. This partnership of materiality and
illusion creates a powerful impact that she has described
as "a sense of anxiety," conveying a demand to enter into

the image despite one's discomfort with the journey.[2] Her
photographs often focus on basic architectural elements
such as stairs, columns, and arches, forms that speak of
passage and structure (see plate 3). By fracturing and
recombining different sites, along with frequently using a
wide-angle lens that makes images seem to envelop and
recede simultaneously, she evokes uncertainty: Will the
structure hold? How stable is the ground? Where do the
paths lead?

Betjemann has described how growing up in an isolated, early eighteenth-century farmhouse gave her a sense
of time as "continuous, with different centuries running
parallel to each other."[3] She also remembers accumulating
boxes of aging postcards of ruins and monuments from
around the world, sent by a father who traveled often for
his job with a shipping company. This recollection is rich
with suggestions of her ongoing themes of the bridges
between distant locations and past times, of decay, and of
absence. Like Eugène Atget's early twentieth-century
photographs of the buildings and streets of Paris, which
are filled with the silence of the past and the unseen,
Betjemann's images suggest lives and events that are outside the camera's vision and the photographic moment.
Their aged feel—the Victorian, sepia-toned quality—in
combination with decaying structures and pervasive
emptiness, evokes time's ravages, while occasional piles of
skulls and bones make clear the association with traditional *vanitas* images that contemplate the fleeting nature
of life.

1. Quoted in Paula Marincola, "Norinne Betjemann: Peeling Back the
Layers of Time," *Moore: A Publication of Moore College of Art and
Design,* Winter 1990, p. 8.
2. Conversation with Kathleen Forde in London, September 21, 1997.
Subsequent unattributed quotes and statements are from this conversation and another with Forde on the previous day.
3. Quoted in Erin Kennedy, "Exhibition Celebrates Photography,"
Philadelphia Inquirer, September 17, 1989, p. H26. (Statement originally printed on the back of a postcard published in a set for the exhibition *The Extended Image* at Ogontz Library Gallery, Pennsylvania
State University, Abington, 1989.)

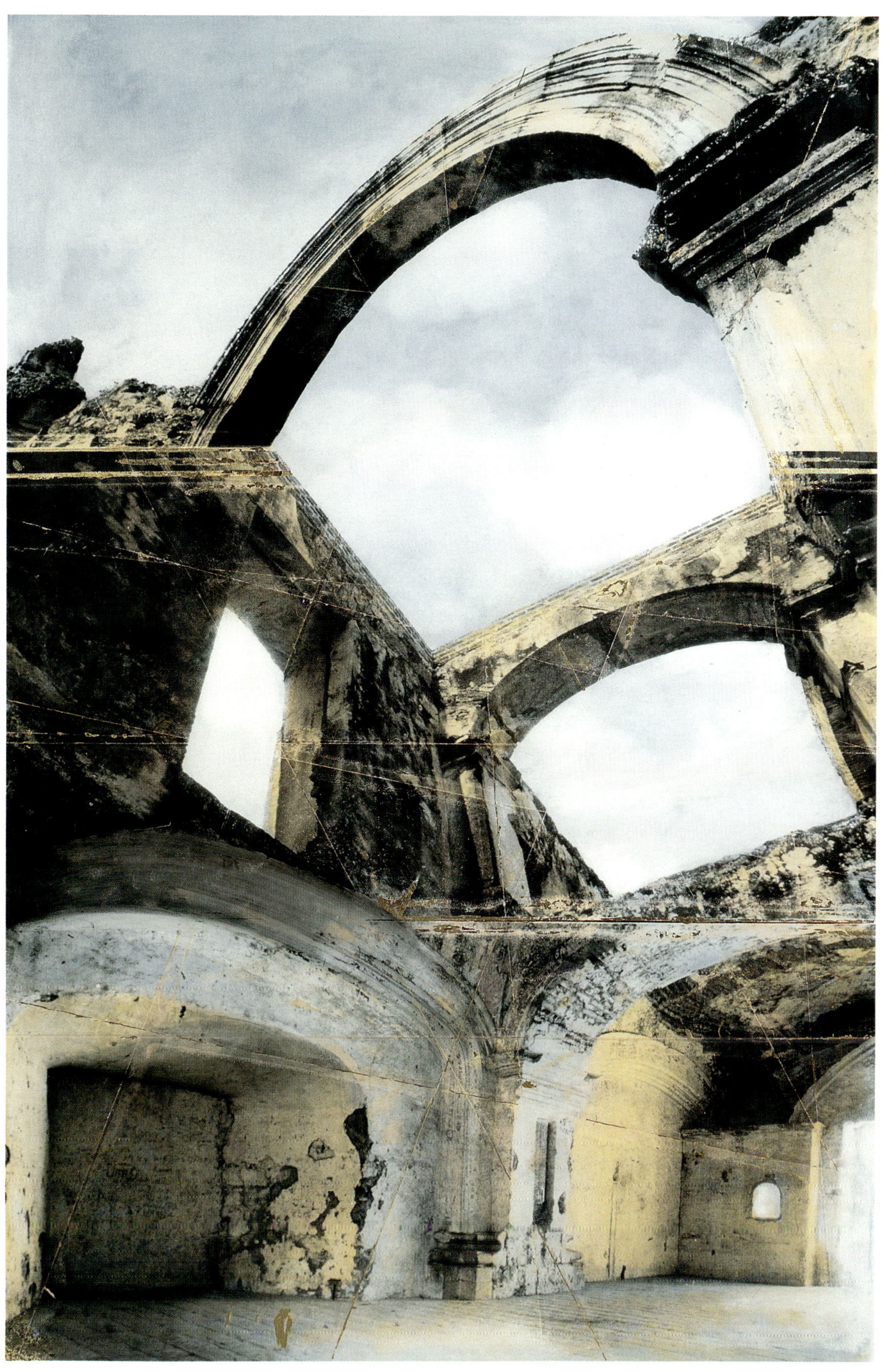

Norinne Betjemann
Freefall, 1989
Photo oils and gold leaf on gelatin silver print
(second from an edition of five)
59 × 38" (149.9 × 96.5 cm)
Collection of Norma and Lawrence Reichlin

Charles Burwell

Throughout his career Charles Burwell's dense, multi-layered paintings and drawings have made the process of their making an evident and integral part of the image. In his early work, up through his 1985 *Challenge* exhibition, Burwell juxtaposed networks of lines, organic shapes, and geometric patterns in amorphous environments that suggested surreal landscapes as much as they remained abstract images. He built up the surfaces of these works with layers of oil stick rubbed between coats in a method akin to traditional glazing. Then, using crayon and pencil, he drew upon these burnished fields, and further scraped and scratched into them with a variety of tools to reveal the underlayers of color and tone. This laborious, multistage process lent these early pieces an intensely handworked appearance and created a warm, atmospheric quality suffused with light.

Burwell's work from the latter half of the 1980s used much the same approach and vocabulary of forms, but intensified the contrasts between light and dark areas and between the figures and the ground so that increasingly distinct organic forms and geometric patterns hovered within even more glowing, richly toned spaces. Throughout the 1980s, Burwell's imagery alluded to cave paintings, fossils, primitive biological forms, and genetic structures, indicating his interests at the time in combining a range of scientific and prehistoric associations. This language of primordial shapes and pictographic markings, in combination with his evolutionary process of making, stirs associations with life's creative processes. With their allusions to multiple layers of time, including biological, geological, and cultural, Burwell's images can be considered as abstract creation stories.

In the early 1990s Burwell's work appeared to change radically, as the dimly lit spaces and evocations of a distant past found in his previous images disappeared. In describing his feelings at the time, Burwell has said that "the romantic quality of the paintings I was making began to be less interesting to me, and there was a sense of nostalgia about the work that I did not like."[1] He started to place forms and patterns more directly over each other in a layering of planes, with mazes, drips, organic forms, and geo-metric patterns seeming to slide past each other in a shallow space. Rather than work back through these layers in his former archaeological manner, he created veils of pattern and allover dispersals of forms through which the underlayers are still visible. In these works, a complex interplay makes figure and ground nearly indistinguishable.

In this body of work, cultural allusions offer a balance to those of nature, and the present replaces the past. The labyrinth serves as an architectural structure rather than an organic form, providing an armature for other elements deriving from electrical charts, maps, plant and cell life, and fingerprint patterns. Burwell's very recent pieces have begun to include occasional representational images such as huts from Southeast Asia and forest scenes taken from *National Geographic* and other popular sources.

In speaking of his long-standing fascination with the forms of written language, which is so evident in the pictographic markings in his early work, Burwell has mentioned cave drawing, Middle Eastern manuscripts, and the paintings of Cy Twombly and Mark Tobey as inspirations. In his newest work, in which he incorporates photographic screenprinting and extensive cutting and reassembling along with conventional drawing methods (see plate 4), the quality of handmade markings is somewhat less evident. Nonetheless, written language continues to be a relevant analogue for Burwell's fine balancing act between abstract form and referential systems, whereby a complex visual pattern of symbols can be read for its wealth of cultural associations.

1. Unpublished artist's statement, c. 1994, Sande Webster Gallery, Philadelphia.

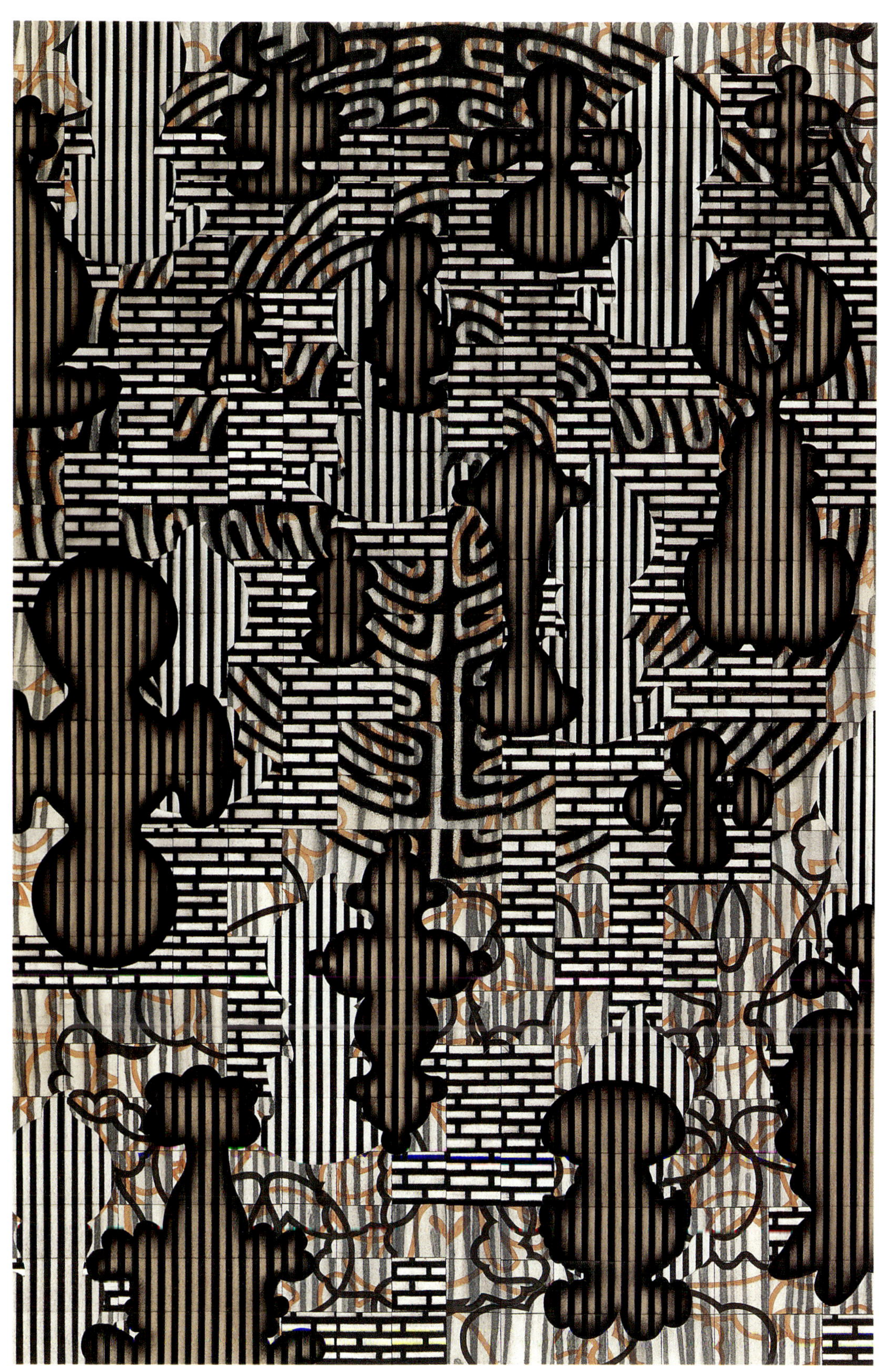

PLATE 4
Charles Burwell
Broken Labyrinth #8, Hybrids, 1997
Watercolor, graphite, pastel, ink, and
tempera on paper
50 × 32" (127 × 81.3 cm)
Collection of the artist, courtesy
Sande Webster Gallery, Philadelphia

Syd Carpenter

Syd Carpenter came to ceramics from painting. She attributes her change of medium to watching Rudolf Staffel work with clay when he taught at the Tyler School of Art. She remembers being "enamored by the beauty of the way clay behaved gesturally" in his hands, an experience that opened her eyes to the expressive possibilities of the ceramic medium.[1]

During the 1980s Carpenter's ceramic work was primarily wall-hung relief sculptures, usually subtly tinted with stains applied before firing. Sometimes she left the natural color of the fired clay to evoke associations with stone and to eliminate distractions from the form. In the early 1990s she began to experiment with more colorful surfaces applied with acrylics after firing, a development whose way was prepared by her training as a painter. While still wall-mounted, these pieces were modeled fully in the round. In addition, the forms were unified wholes rather than the sequences of abutting forms that preceded them.

The human figure has always been a central element in Carpenter's sculptures. In the early pieces the body often appeared as semiabstract but recognizable fragments in the overall sequence of images. During the mid-1990s, when her work was at its most abstract, the human figure was represented by stand-ins such as vessels, bottles, and rootlike forms. Her most recent pieces have returned full circle to her earliest work by including fully recognizable, naturalistic representations of the figure, often based on Carpenter's mind's-eye images of herself and her mother.

Carpenter's pieces have always been amalgams of forms deriving from a variety of sources, including industrial objects, plants, animals, and natural elements such as water. She has mentioned the importance of gardening as inspiration, as can be readily seen in the proliferation of roots, vines, and branches. Other elements grow out of her notebook sketches, where abstract shapes deriving from the gestures of the hand—shapes that couldn't easily be sketched in clay—become sources for translation into her sculptural medium.

While Carpenter's forms draw on various sources, the wellspring for her pieces is always a word or phrase—its sound and texture along with its associated images, mean-ings, and emotions. The organic and inorganic models she uses are the means by which she seeks to translate language into material form. In early pieces she alluded to this foundation in language by joining a sequence of forms to produce a narrative flow, whereas in later works the connection between parts is more seamless, although the relationship between dissimilar elements is still an essential component.

This working method often produces sculptures with the feeling of personal allegory. Carpenter considers *Still Processing* (plate 5), for example, to be a self-portrait, a symbolic representation of her own process of distilling a lifetime of memories and information. The knot of raw experience at the top, full of remembered objects of daily life, leads through the large, twisting cord to the oversized bottle. The piece's sanguine color and suggestions of internal plumbing allude to the human subject, a reference underscored by the traditional symbolism of the female as a vessel, here overturned.

Carpenter's innovative forms stretch the conventional expectations of ceramics as solidly grounded, stable-footed objects. She feels a freedom to make clay do what it does not do naturally—to twist and turn, bear paint, and defy gravity—thereby creating a sense of risk and vitality in her sculpture. As she has explained, "I'm interested in the material and I'm not married to a tradition. I didn't start doing clay because I thought that I was going to contribute to some tradition that had to do with glazes and firing and the whole dialogue. My association with clay is because I like the way this material behaves in response to the ideas that I bring to it."

1. Conversation with the author, May 29, 1997. All subsequent quotes and references are taken from this discussion and one on August 22, 1997.

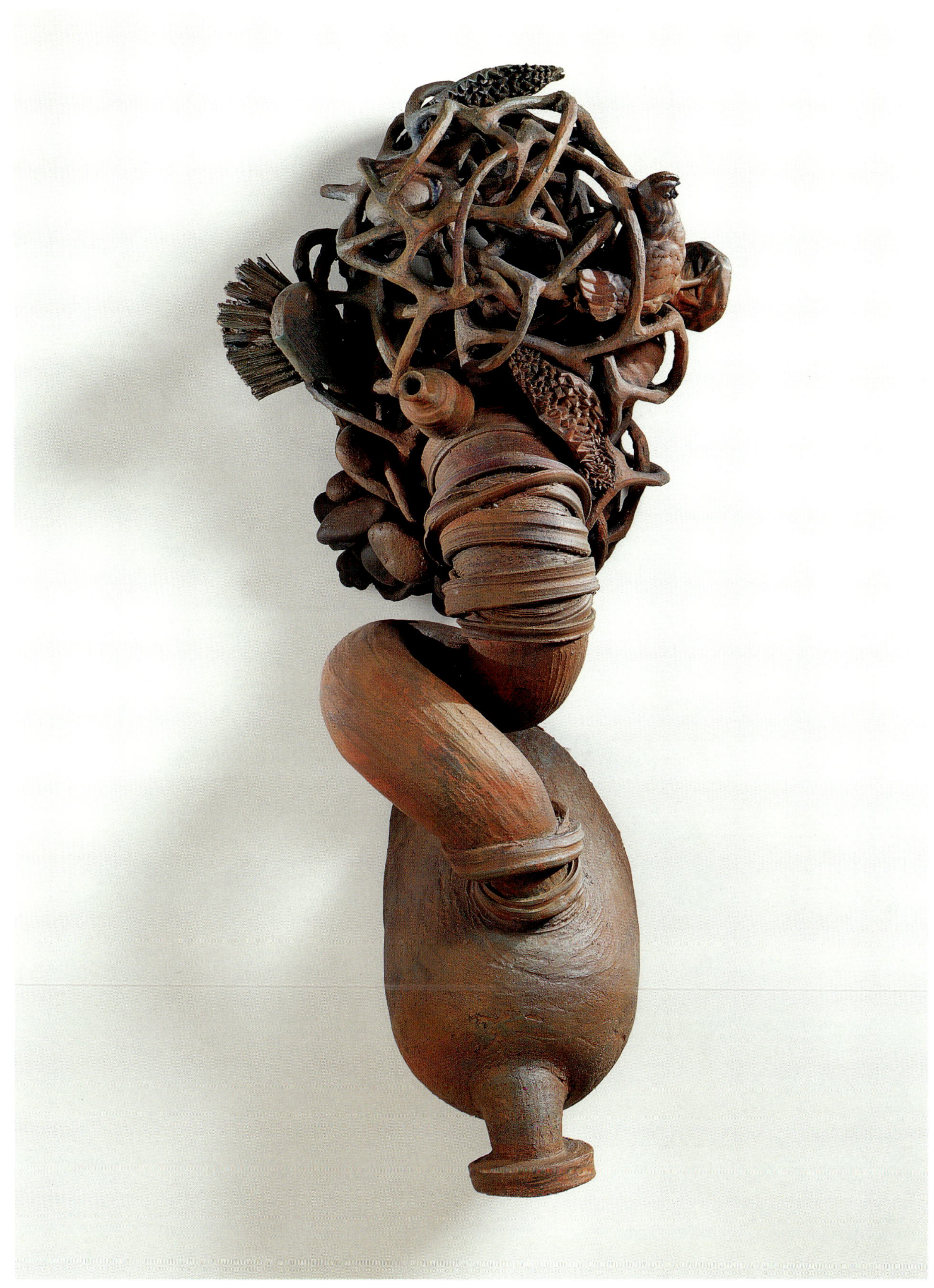

Syd Carpenter
Still Processing, 1994
Acrylic on earthenware with stones,
painted wood brush, and plaster
50 × 18 × 10" (127 × 45.7 × 25.4 cm)
Collection of the artist, courtesy
Sande Webster Gallery, Philadelphia

Frank Galuszka

Over the past twenty years, Frank Galuszka's painting has ranged from detailed realism to thickly painted abstraction. Until the late 1980s, his work involved lush narratives marked by vivid, saturated colors, fully modeled figures in convincing spaces, and detailed rendering of objects. These scenes mostly depict single or multiple figures either in interiors or outdoors in shallow, stagelike foregrounds before glimpses into the distance. They are characterized by moods of stillness, as solitary figures seem to dream, watch, or wait. Communication between figures is caught in a moment of suspension, evident only in a glance or attitude of attention. These are narratives ripe with portent, as if the painting itself were thinking.

In the late 1980s, the surface of Galuszka's paintings began to break up into dense screens of brightly colored paint, what he calls "exploded cellular near-abstraction."[1] While the predominant effect was that of paint—thick, intense accumulations—these works were never fully abstract, as they contained barely discernible representations of figures and objects, and collaged items such as a coffee-cup lid or bits of reflective mica that enhance the active, shimmering quality of the surface. The buildup of surface incident around these details of reality suggests analogues for an overstimulated vision, as if the image recorded a hallucinatory experience of the visible world.

Galuszka understands these two periods in his work as expressions of the same underlying concerns rather than a simple opposition of figuration and abstraction. In his early narrative works Galuszka's carefully considered attention to form and composition gave them a highly constructed appearance, beyond an easy naturalism. In his later abstract paintings the elaborate working of every bit of the surface results in a high level of variety and intensity that leads us to understand his abstract images as strongly allegorical and bursting with possible meanings. Work from the mid-1990s returns to naturalistic figures, but places them in abstract settings, further complicating the idea of a linear progression from representational to nonobjective (see figure 9).

Throughout his career, Galuszka's images have been motivated by textual associations. He often combines classical, mythological, and biblical sources with contemporary figures and settings. In *Bethany* (plate 6), two women in modern dress allude to Mary and Martha from Bethany, who in the biblical story called upon Jesus to raise their brother Lazarus from the dead. In the painting, a man's reflection, perhaps alluding to the returning Lazarus, appears in the window. As with many of Galuszka's works, an aura of the past seems to pervade, even comment on, the present, regardless of whether one grasps the narrative allusion. Galuszka says that he has his own "long reverie about what the painting is about . . . [but] this does not mean at all that I want anyone else to think that this is what the painting is about." He further explains, "I try to paint paintings that have enough ingredients in them to result in a good story, but not in such a way that they determine what the story is. For me, two readings of this painting are both equally legitimate."

1. Artist's lecture at the University of the Arts, Philadelphia, July 23, 1997. Subsequent quotes are from this lecture and from conversations with the artist on May 5 and September 4, 1997.

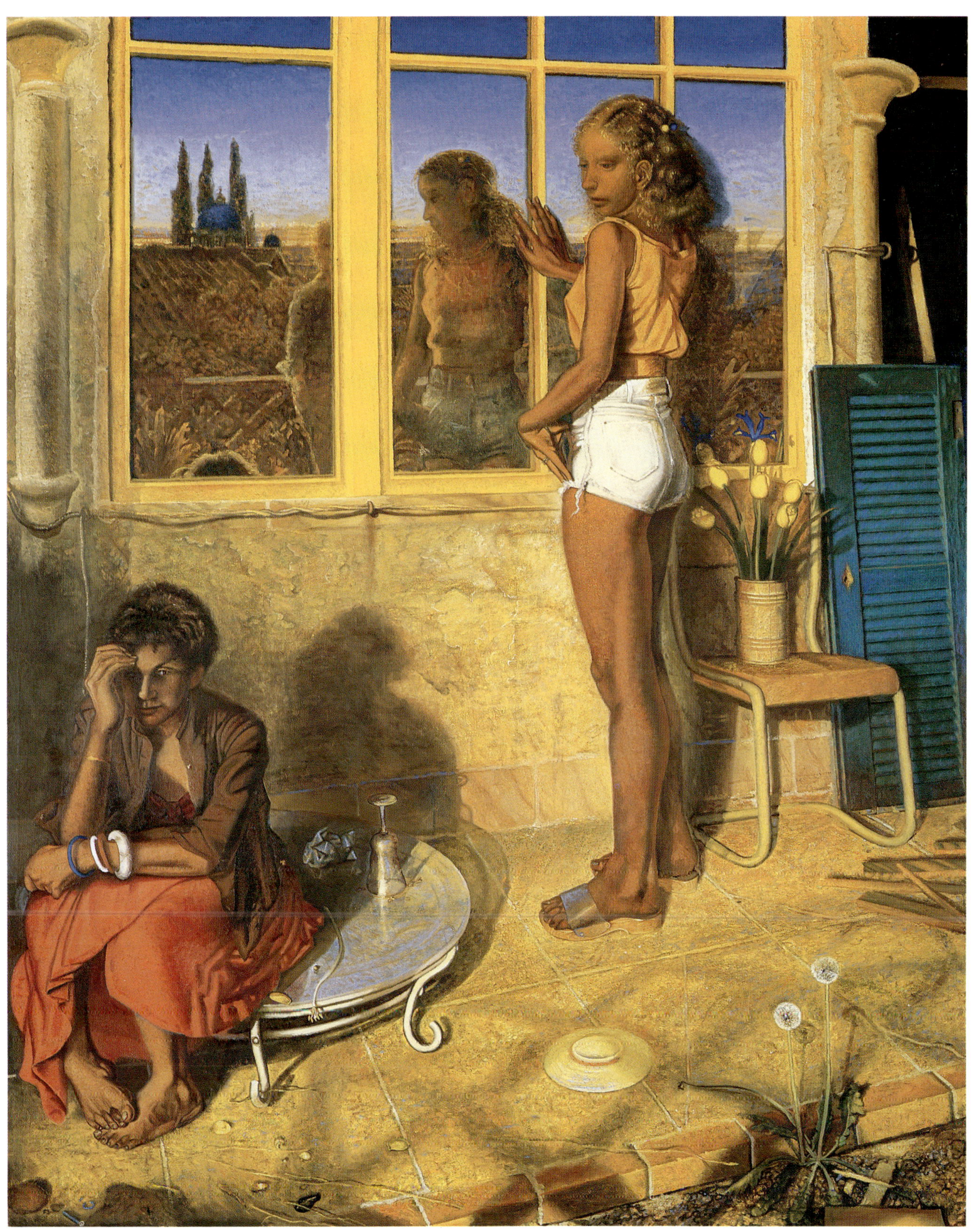

Frank Galuszka
Bethany, 1979–82
Oil on canvas
102 × 80¾" (259.1 × 205.1 cm)
Collection of the artist, courtesy
The More Gallery, Inc., Philadelphia

Michael Grothusen

Michael Grothusen is a sculptor, in an expanded sense of the term, for while he does make discrete, freestanding objects, he prefers to make sculptural installations that intervene in architectural settings. One early piece, *Shim* (1991), bridged the space of the Tyler Gallery in center-city Philadelphia without touching the floor. Grothusen had wedged together pieces of scrap wood to form an arc held aloft by the architectural principle of the keystone, which transforms the pull of gravity into upward lift. He drove smaller shims in between the slats and wetted the whole each day, increasing its lateral pressure on the side walls of the gallery. Not inadvertently, it recalled Chris Burden's famous piece *Samson* of 1985 (private collection), in which wooden beams were slowly ratcheted into the gallery walls by each visitor who came through the turnstile entrance.

Before turning to sculpture, Grothusen studied architecture and strongly considered entering that profession. In addition to employing its structural principles, as in *Shim,* he frequently uses materials from abandoned houses that speak of our architectural heritage and the values that buildings embody. Some recent pieces have used more contemporary building materials, including vinyl siding and fiberglass insulation. The forms of his pieces, too, often resemble houses, bridges, ships, and other inhabitable or utilitarian structures.

A primary concern of Grothusen's work is the dialogue between sculpture and its surrounding space. For this exhibition Grothusen has made a new work that responds to the architecture of the Philadelphia Museum of Art. Inspired by a vintage postcard of massive columns being hoisted into place during the construction of the Cleveland Museum of Art in 1914, he has built a cratelike structure that has been affixed to a column in the Museum's Great Stair Hall, thereby asking us to consider the interplay of sculpture and architecture by an imagined narrative of construction or deconstruction (see plate 7).

The movement in sculpture away from objects and toward installations that respond to their site was encouraged while Grothusen was a graduate student at the Tyler School of Art. He credits his teachers Winifred Lutz and Amy Hauft, both sculptors and installation artists, with steering students in this direction. Grothusen also notes that the experience of his residency at the Skowhegan School of Painting and Sculpture in 1991 inclined him to the idea of temporary work, which he explored by making *Ice House,* a latticed structure held together by having its tension lines embedded in two three-hundred-pound blocks of slowly melting ice.

By making his pieces responsive to selected features of a specific site, Grothusen hopes to encourage the viewer to develop a heightened awareness of one's own place in that environment. This emphasis on the experience of viewing—a phenomenological approach to content—is a legacy of Minimalist sculpture of the 1960s, in which simple, often industrially manufactured forms were partly intended to draw the viewer's attention to him- or herself in the act of observing these forms. Grothusen, like so many sculptors working in a post-Minimalist context, marries these concerns to other issues. By his use of familiar building materials, his semirepresentational forms, and the evidence of his hand labor, he seeks an expanded range of reference to the world outside of the immediate viewing experience, one that also embraces individual and cultural memory.

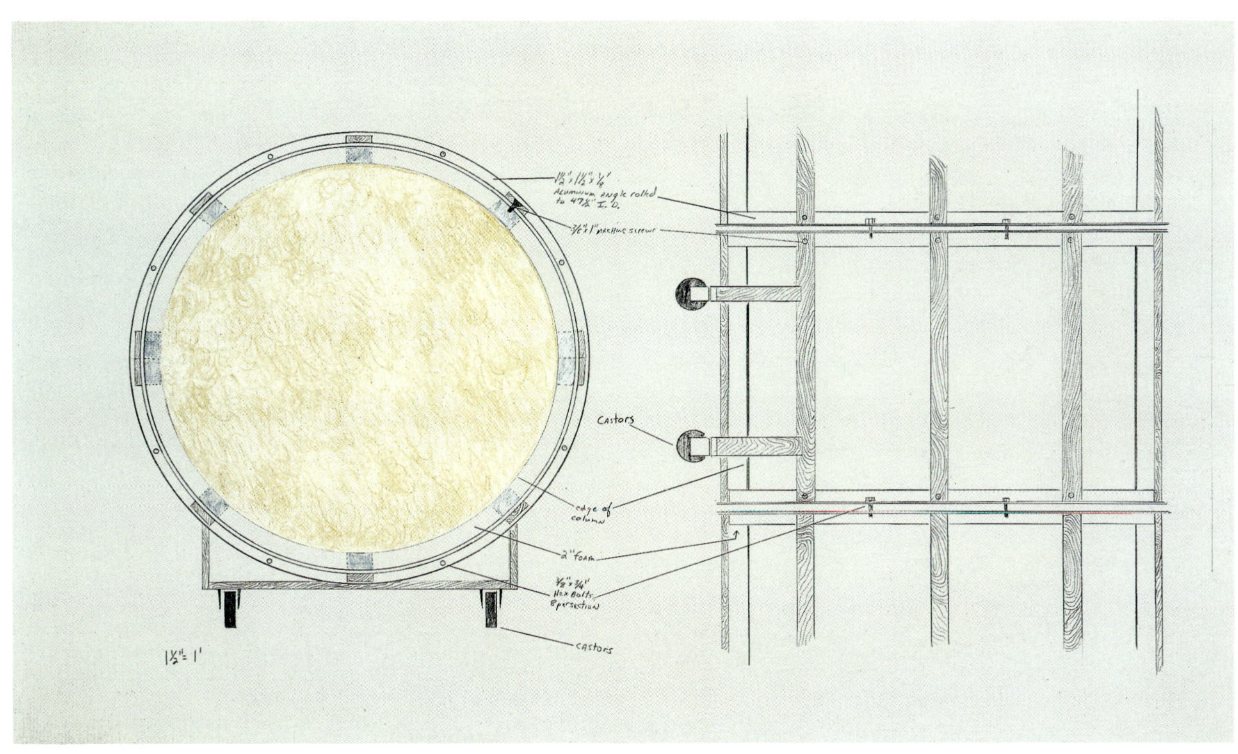

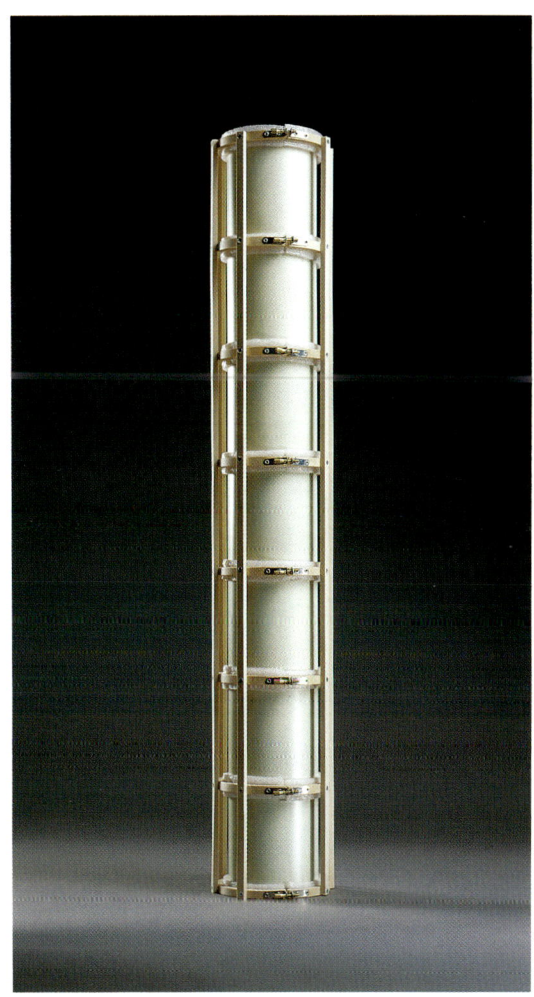

Michael Grothusen
Drawing and maquette
for *Moving the Museum,*
an installation at the
Philadelphia Museum of Art, 1998

Mei-ling Hom

While she began her career as a ceramicist, Mei-ling Hom rather quickly moved into multimedia sculptures and installations. Even at the beginning, her allegiances were not so much to the clay medium and its traditions as to the themes and concepts that still guide her work and that involve a wide range of materials and forms for their expression. While no one signature style unites her various installations, her work is characterized by an orderliness, refinement, and austere sensuousness.

Hom's pieces often invite viewers to participate directly by passing through or over them. An early piece, *Bridge* (1985), consisted of a beam placed over a brook and split lengthwise to bend outward, forcing one to traverse it bow-legged. In *Going Green* of 1988 (figure 3), an installation in Philadelphia's Fairmount Park, viewers entered a structure on a narrow path between vines of morning glories and beneath an arcade of sprinkler tubes. The sprinklers came on periodically to form arcs of spray and rainbows above the growing vines, enclosing viewers in a continually changing environment.

Since about 1990, Hom's interest in the experiences of Asians in the United States in general and in her own Chinese heritage in particular has become a central theme in her work, extending her concern with physical space to the notion of cultural space. During a residency in 1990 at the Headlands Center for the Arts north of San Francisco, she became acutely aware of seeing Asians on the West Coast integrated into all levels of society rather than limited to the restaurant, grocery store, and laundry roles familiar to her from New Haven and Philadelphia. For her Headlands installation Hom created a ceremonial walkway with Asian cooking utensils attached to super-sized chopsticks. The path led to gray, translucent curtains made of large sheets of the material used to add substance to shirt collars, which also recalled the early morning fog that shrouds the Marin County coast where the art center is located.

For another work, a collaborative, community-based project called *Picturing Asian America,* realized in San Francisco in 1993 and in Philadelphia the following year, Hom distributed disposable cameras to one hundred peo-ple of all ages from a full range of Asian backgrounds. Hom asked her collaborators to photograph the people, places, and events in their lives that best expressed their ethnic identity. The results were exhibited in a gallery setting and as sets of postcards, with short texts written by the photographers.

For the Philadelphia Museum of Art's exhibition, Hom created *Golden Mountain,* a large, saffron-colored sculpture for one of the galleries of twentieth-century American art (see plate 8). Covering the surface of her piece, hundreds of tiny eyes look out at the art of Western culture. Noting that the Chinese term for "America" translates as "Golden Mountain," she has merged the idea of Western riches with an Eastern spiritual dimension, as she derived the figure from the mountainlike forms of huge meditating Buddha sculptures.

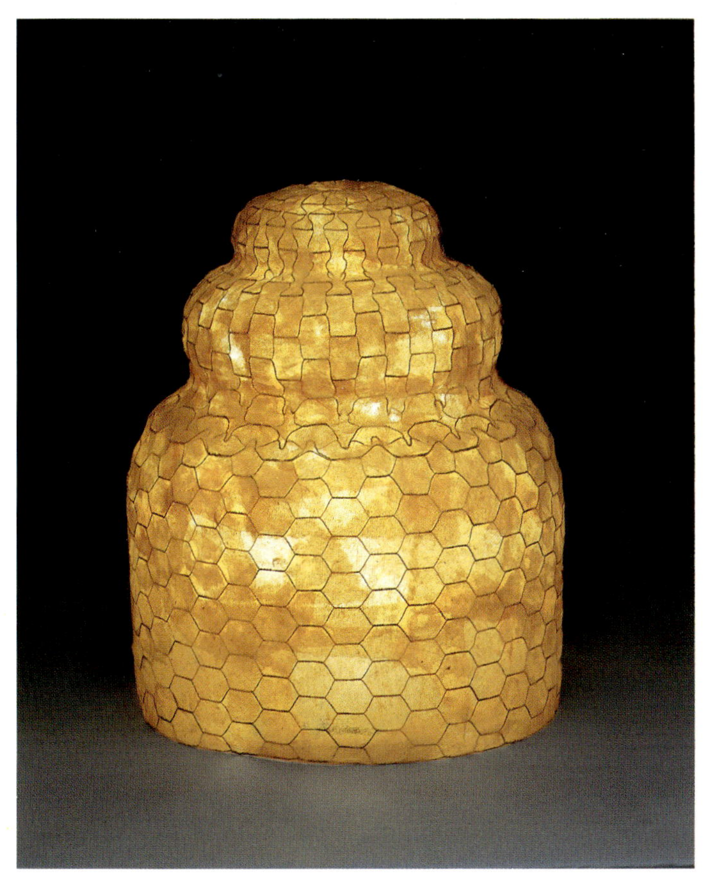

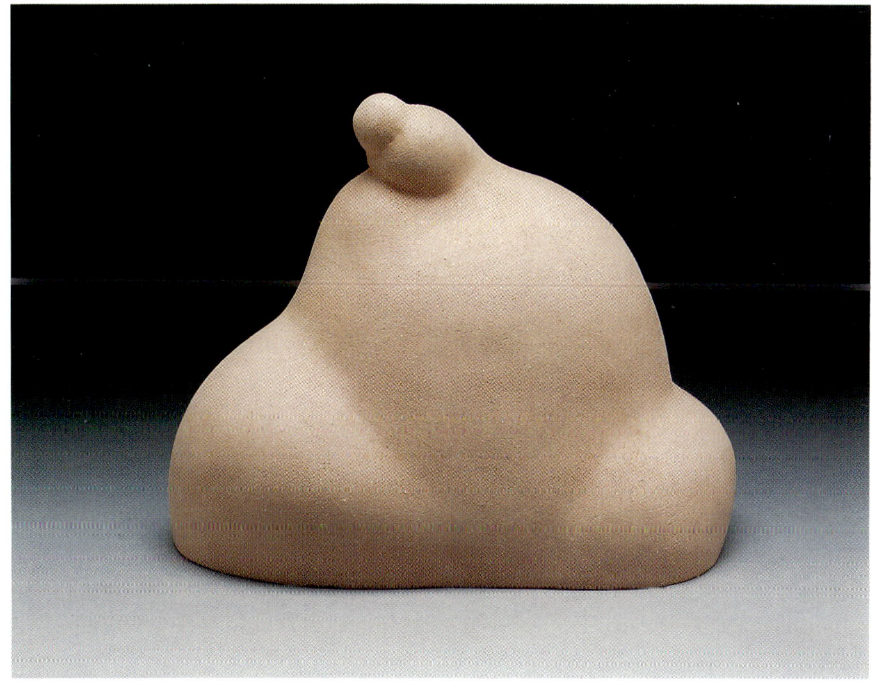

PLATE 8
Mei-ling Hom
Maquettes for *Golden Mountain,* an installation
at the Philadelphia Museum of Art, 1998

Stacy Levy

A background in forestry and environmental science has led Stacy Levy to make art that applies the language of science to natural phenomena. She uses methods such as quantifying, categorizing, and magnifying as ways to make the normally invisible processes of nature visible and already visible phenomena coherent. A list of some of her titles indicates her approach: *A Month of Tides, Leaf Tally, Calendar of Rain,* and *Seeing the Path of the Wind* (figure 5).

Although Levy continues to make independent objects, her works primarily take the form of installations and, increasingly, public outdoor commissions.[1] For a 1991 show at the Moore College of Art and Design in Philadelphia she used one thousand tiny organza flags to chart the course of the wind as it blew across a weathervane and anemometer on top of the building and relayed data to changeable electric fans in the gallery (see figure 5). For a 1993 exhibition at Miami-Dade Community College, she constructed a sixty-foot-tall, collapsible fabric tower that rose and fell with the tides in nearby Biscayne Bay. Pieces such as these take place in real time, tracking natural processes as they unfold at their actual pace. The lucidity of her works creates the sense that nature is embodying itself in the forms and materials that she presents, making it easy to forget that her installations are reinventions of these processes, translations of phenomena that already have forms.

Levy generally uses common, nonart materials in her installations, and they function in ways not all that different from their everyday use. In *Hidden River* (plate 9), for example, she built an accurate map of the Schuylkill River, from its headwaters in east-central Pennsylvania to its mouth in the Delaware River, using galvanized plumbing pipes, found porcelain sinks, and running water. The four major cities drawing their drinking water from the river are each represented by a sink hung on the wall whose cold-water line feeds from the waste pipe of the "upriver" sink, a graphic display of shared water resources. In other pieces Levy has used paper shipping tags, plastic cups, rain and river water, and glass jars. The status of these everyday materials is thus elevated not merely by the Duchampian tactic of having been selected by the artist to be art, but also by the role they play in illuminating larger social issues in an elegantly simple way.

Levy's interest in environmental installations builds on the genre of earthworks—also known as earth art or environmental art—initiated by artists in the 1960s and 1970s. Constructed out in nature, often at remote sites, earthworks are mostly known to audiences through photographic documentation presented in a gallery or museum. They often share a methodology of superimposing on nature human constructs, such as measurement, as a way to illuminate the intersection of human and natural laws and processes. Levy's work, too, sets up a dialogue between nature and culture and frequently creates an active relationship between a representation in a gallery setting and a natural source or event outside. She has noted that "the twentieth century has employed the scientist as the translator of nature. Yet science uses a limited vocabulary and is often a language of separation, rather than incorporation."[2] Levy, then, applies her methods of ordering, counting, and sampling not to achieve accuracy and objectivity but, as she describes, "to formulate another way of seeing, in which the viewer is both observing and experiencing the natural world."[3]

1. Levy is currently working with Winifred Lutz and Mierle Laderman Ukeles on a public installation for Philadelphia's planned Schuylkill River Park.
2. Quoted in *Pew Fellowships in the Arts, 1991–92* (Philadelphia, 1993), n.p.
3. Quoted in Rosenwald-Wolf Gallery, University of the Arts, Philadelphia, *Stacy Levy: Watercourse* (March 8–April 21, 1996), n.p.

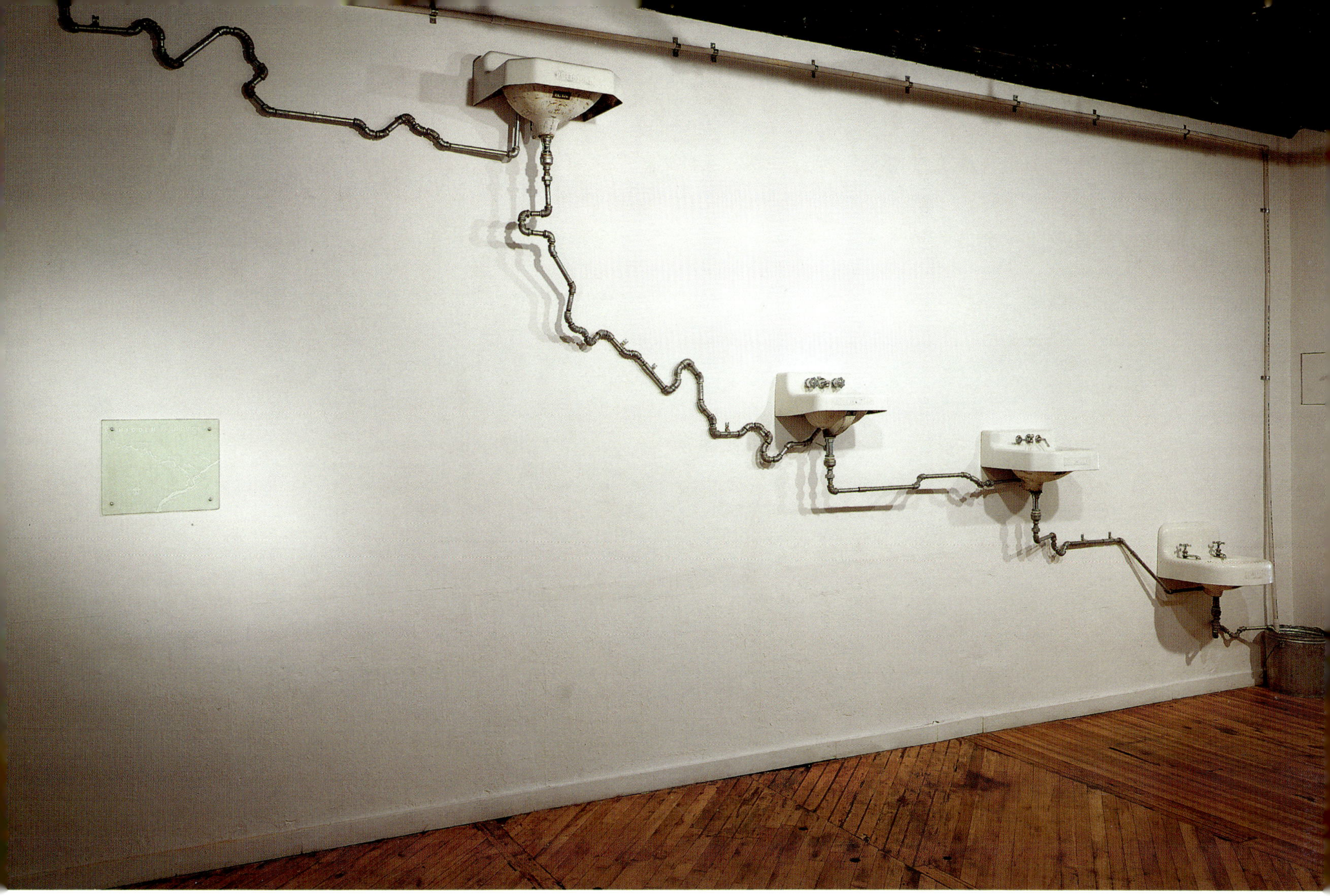

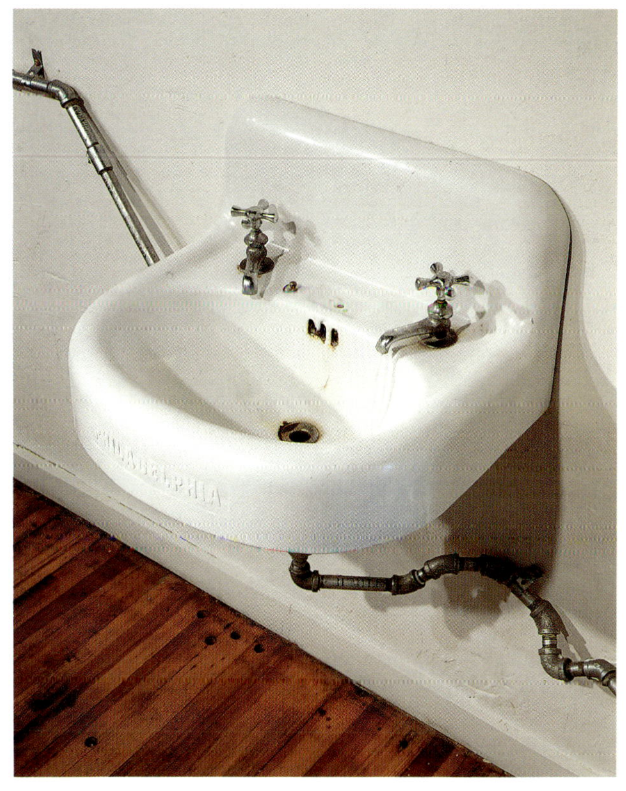

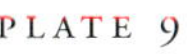

PLATE 9

Stacy Levy

Hidden River, 1990
Galvanized pipe, porcelain sinks,
water, sandblasted glass, PVC pipe,
vinyl letters, and water pump
15 × 30 × 2½' (4.6 × 9.1 × 0.8 m)
Courtesy Fairmount Water Works
Interpretive Center, Philadelphia
Water Department

Tristin Lowe

Tristin Lowe's art is a theatrical mix of crude materials, leftovers, and low-tech solutions, a jerry-built art of inflatable figures, beds that wet themselves, and clowns propelled by model rockets. It has been remarked that his art dwells on the absurdity of existence with a Beckett-like aimlessness.[1] Lowe is drawn to images and figures from the margins of society, the fools and tricksters who embody his recurring themes of vulgarity and play, vulnerability and failure.

Lowe has often identified himself with the clown, portraying this figure as his muse or angel. The clown first appeared in his art in the early 1990s. Lowe was moving away from more formalist work based on the well-crafted use of traditional sculpture materials, and found himself carving heads out of plaster and constructing bodies from balloons and other found parts. He imagines the clown, in his willingness to make a fool of himself, as being able to transcend his reality to achieve the nirvana of the Buddha. But as an emblem of humiliating self-exposure, the clown can also represent one's worst fears, and Lowe's work often embraces the things that most terrify him.

A brutal honesty marks Lowe's art, in which an idea stands or falls on its own merits without recourse to embellishments. He leaves visible the mechanics of his installations—the motors, electrical cords, work lamps, and tension wires, all of which have their own formal appeal. As Lowe has said, "I want what makes it look like art to be the means, the trying, the idea."[2] This unadorned, bare-bones aesthetic also contains moments of delicate beauty. A silk balloon surmounted by a tiny head gently expands and deflates in response to the motion of passersby; a multi-layered plastic "big top" is forlornly lit by a single bare bulb (see figure 6); a pattern of concentric water stains on a blue satiny mattress marks the ebbs and flows of the puddle made by a small fountain in its middle.

Lowe's insistence on revealing the skeleton along with the skin is far from a refusal to create illusion. His figures and props spin psychological dreamscapes that resonate with what he describes as the "marvelous merry thoughts of joining the circus" as well as the "harsh reality, the melancholy, forlorn sadness" that often accompany this.

His work surprises in the range of associations prompted by so spare and elusive a presentation, as if the meanings existed in the gap between what is suggested and what is actually present. Lowe has explained, "I'm not very interested in telling something in a cut-and-dried way. I'm more interested in getting you to a place or a mood or a feeling that you are going to try to figure out, . . . in that type of resonance or awkwardness that makes you mull it over, hopefully more than once." Lowe's installation made for this exhibition extends his provocative amalgams of childhood innocence and knowing experience (see plate 10). A giant, inflatable "Alice" doll looms over one of the galleries of twentieth-century art, her head bent forward by the ceiling. A single, oversized eyeball fills her face, muting her other senses and suggesting her glimpse into another reality.

1. Edward J. Sozanski, "Talkin' at ICA: What Is One to Say?" *Philadelphia Inquirer,* May 26, 1996, p. D9.
2. Conversation with the author, March 21, 1997. Subsequent quotations are from the same conversation.

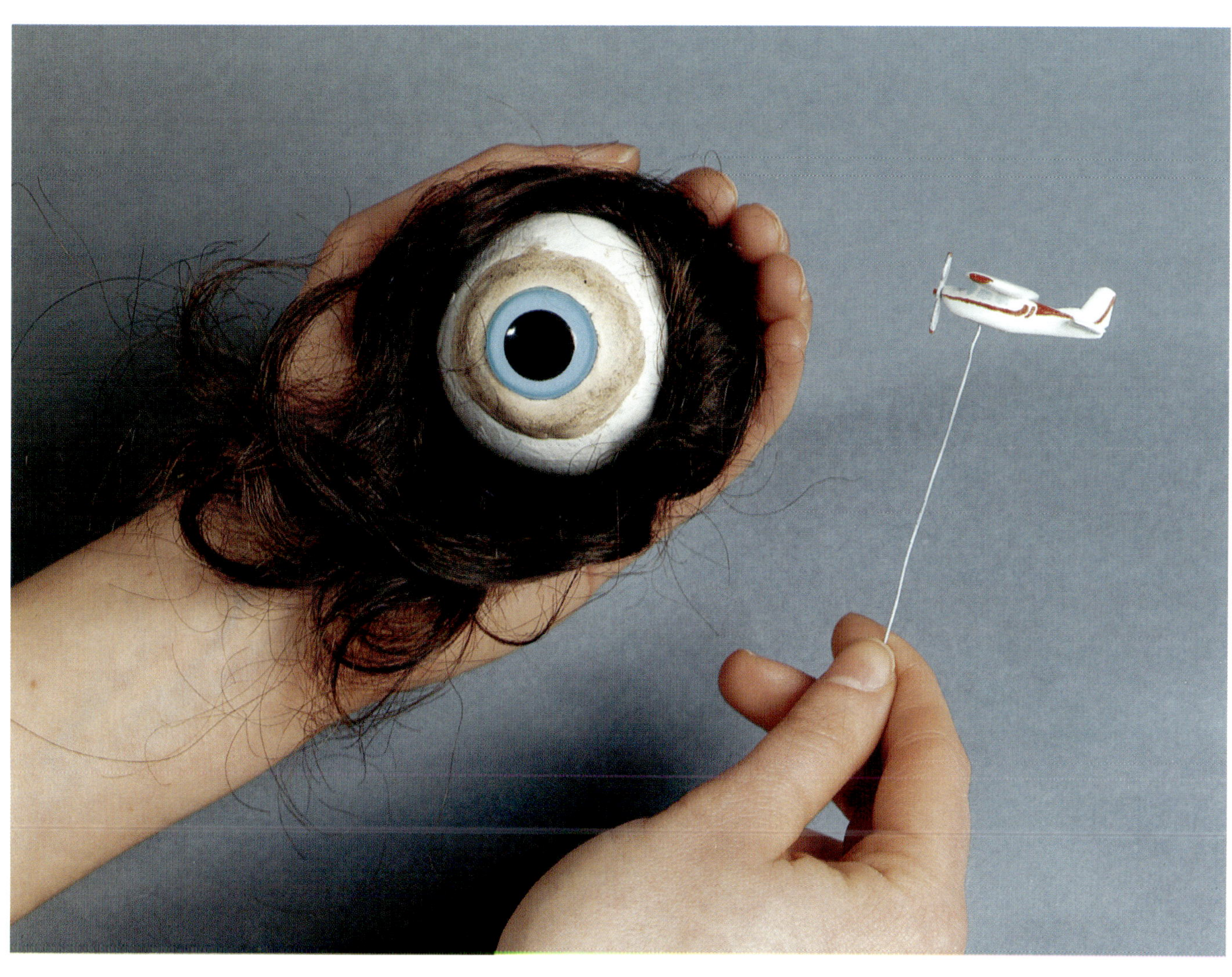

Tristin Lowe

"Sketch" for *Alice*, an installation at the
Philadelphia Museum of Art, 1998

Gabriel Martinez

Excruciating self-exposure drives Gabriel Martinez's work. In photography and performance, he displays what we usually try to hide. He has shown images of the rashes, pimples, and stretch marks on his naked body in large, color light boxes commonly used for bus shelter advertising (see figure 12). He has also mounted details of his body on extension and tabletop mirrors, mimicking the self-scrutiny that these devices assist. Perhaps most startling, in a 1995 performance at White Columns in New York, he submerged his naked body in a narrow, vertical glass tank filled with water, vulnerably placing himself on live display as he breathed through a snorkel.

For Martinez, minor physical imperfections are the stuff of major critique; they enable him to hold up a mirror to a cultural obsession with personal appearance and surface perfection. As a gay man, Martinez can reflect on gay culture's version of this societal preoccupation, which includes aspects of both pride and self-punishment.

Photography, as a medium based on exposure, is a perfect vehicle for Martinez's concerns. The photograph is made by exposing sensitive film to light, and its results hold a special claim to representing reality. It can bring a clarity of detail to bear on the activity of scrutinizing the visible surface, which Martinez furthers by his frequent use of a large-format, eight-by-ten-inch camera. His assertive, even confrontational use of photography to engage issues of identity, media influence, and the body as an ideological construct reflects a general trend in photography of the late 1980s and 1990s. In addition, his photographs have the cold quality of the plastic surgeon's documents that he saw regularly at an early job at a film-processing chain as well as the glamour of advertising.

Martinez's work embraces both mortification and courage. His cheeky acceptance of vanity and self-absorption is what allows him to comment on these conditions from within. In addition to critique, Martinez's approach serves a cathartic function. "The more I release, the more I want to release," he has said. "The more I experience the crucible of humiliating exposure of imperfection, the more I want to continue on that path . . . for the purifying, therapeutic, cleansing feeling of . . . coming clean."[1]

Martinez's strategy of self-exposure has led him to consider the related issues of the male gaze and desire, two themes that are central to contemporary art theory and criticism. His images are strongly related to the age-old tradition of representing the nude body as an object. But by using his own, male body as an object of both desire and repulsion, Martinez complicates the notion of the male gaze. He is at the same time the subject and object of his work, the looker and the looked-at. From his dual perspective, he represents both the dominant culture of masculinity with its objectifying gaze and the "Other" of homosexuality.

In a recent series, Martinez focused on one hundred heterosexual male sitters (plate 11). Using a nineteenth-century technique called ambrotype, in which photographs are printed on small glass plates, he made tiny, exquisite images of the feet and lower legs of his subjects, each of whom was left alone to activate the camera's shutter release at the moment of autoerotic climax. As the instigator, collector, and presenter of the records of these private events, Martinez turns the male gaze back on itself. Moreover, seen as a whole, this series establishes an unexpected resonance between sexuality and spirituality as the partially contained figures suggest traditional Christian images of ascension.

1. Conversation with the author, April 1, 1997.

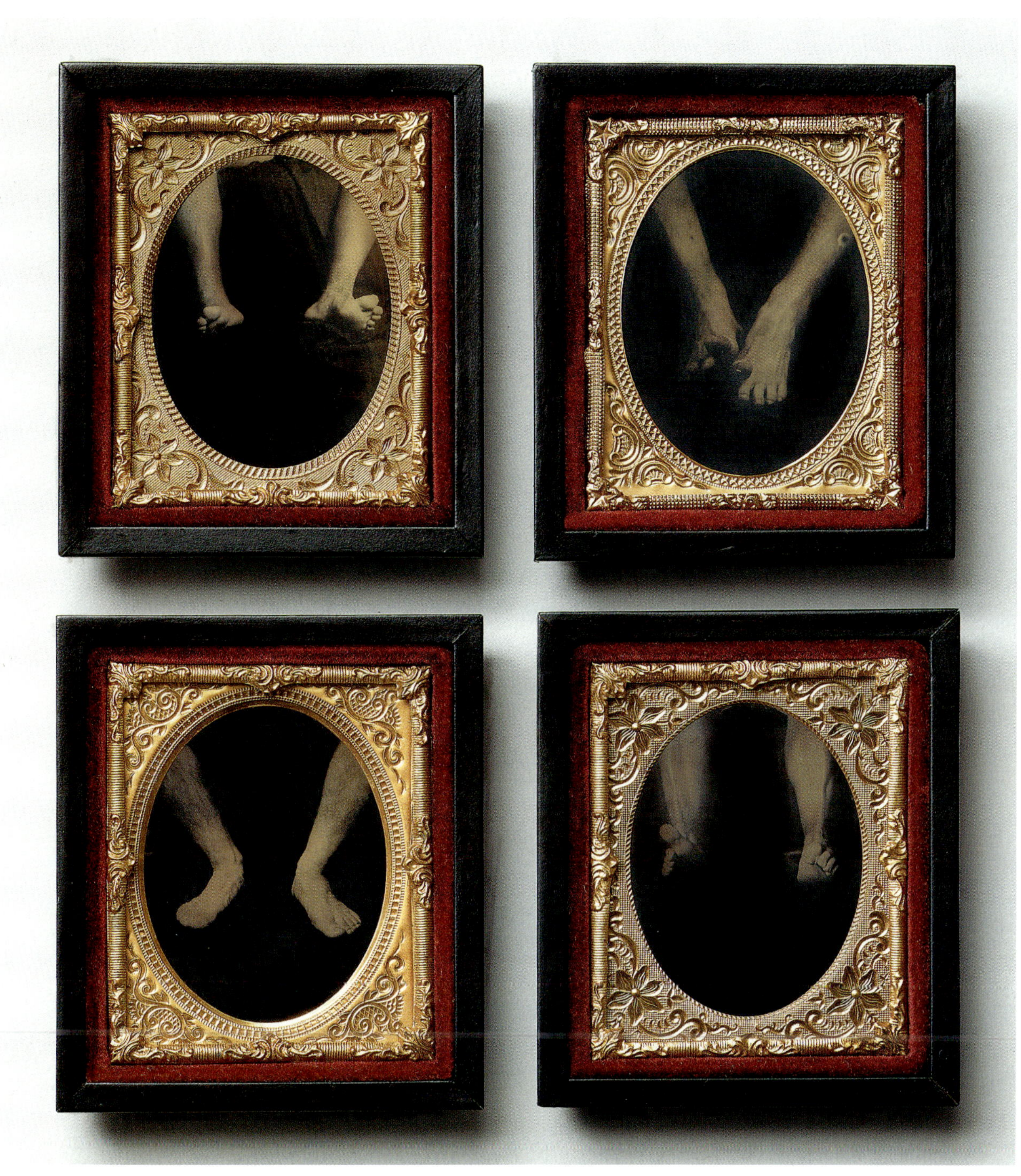

Gabriel Martinez
Adam, Philip, Martin, and *David*
(clockwise from upper left), 1996–98
Tintype prototypes for *Self-Portraits by
Heterosexual Men* (see checklist 24)
3 × 2⅝" (7.6 × 6.7 cm) each
Collection of the artist

Susan Moore

Susan Moore is best known for her monumental likenesses of unnamed individuals. Painted as large as seven-feet square, these imposing, confrontational portraits are at once specific people and generalized landscapes of the face that offer no access to the person's interior life. The subjects may avert our gaze by looking off into the distance or stare back at us with masklike expressions (see figure 10). Moore also paints on a smaller scale, presenting her faces in groups to emphasize their similarities and differences.

Moore's work balances representation and abstraction. Using traditional painting techniques, she slowly builds up her images with layers of underpainting to make solid illusions of volumetric figures inhabiting space. At the same time she undermines her illusions by exaggerating the properties of her working method. As she works, bits of the oil stick and pastel that are her primary mediums break off and accumulate in uneven deposits, creating a thick, multicolor crust of paint. This pitted surface reads as the skin of both the painting and the figure, establishing a tension between portraiture and the two-dimensional surface. She adds to this tension by using bold, sometimes unnatural colors, by tightly cropping the figures within the frame, and by making strong shadows fall across the faces.

The artist says that she chooses her subjects for their eyes. She looks for what she describes as "a clarity of looking that is at the same time vacant, where the expression . . . is absent."[1] She photographs her models in a strong raking light that makes it difficult for them to see. Then she enhances their stare in her paintings by enlarging their eyes. Her sitters' lack of engagement and expression allows viewers to inject their own sense of the person into the image, to make the image anything they want. Moore's recent paintings, however, have strengthened the connection to the individual sitters by including their names in the titles. She has also become more interested in the particularity of different facial types and has broadened the range of models to include more men and a wider range of ages and ethnic identities.[2]

Since the early 1980s Moore has also painted backs, a subject that, in its concealment of individual identity, may initially seem the antithesis of the face. In many ways, however, both groups concern the same issues, and provide information about the subject based on body type and pose. An early series of small, tightly painted backs from her 1982 *Challenge* exhibition places Moore herself, painted with the aid of two mirrors, in shallow spaces before backdrops. Moore based some of her poses on classical and Renaissance sculpture, including the *Dying Niobid*, who pulls an arrow out of her back, and Donatello's *David.* Subsequent back paintings, including a large series completed in 1995, entitled *Back Portraits*, simplify the poses and environments in favor of emphasizing light and dark contrasts and a more heavily textured surface (plate 12).

Moore continues to look to past art for inspiration. A series of faces from the early 1990s, made after a sojourn in Italy, have the lucidity and crisp palette of Renaissance frescoes. Her interest in late Egyptian burial portraits inspired her recent use of gold paint-stick. She is also fascinated by early Greek and Egyptian statuary, and it is not hard to see why, since her own work shares with those rigidly frontal sculptures a tension between individuality and generality—an aloof otherworldliness informed by a powerful sense of life.

1. Conversation with the author, May 27, 1997. All subsequent quotes are from this and other conversations in September and October 1997.
2. This increased emphasis on individuality was prompted in part by using her children as sitters, an experience that led her to think of all of her portraits as being of particular people.

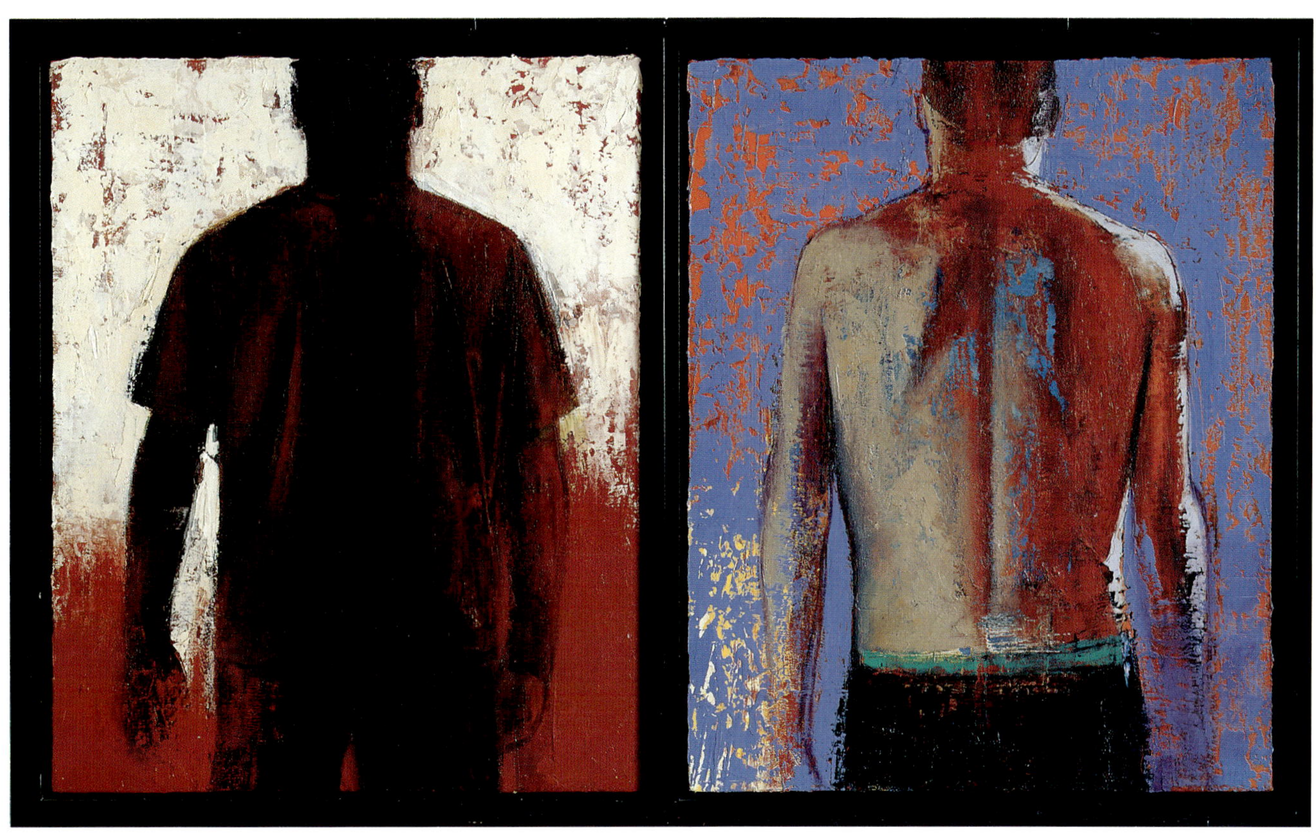

PLATE 12

Susan Moore

Back Portraits, 1995

Oil on canvas

32 × 20" (81.3 × 50.8 cm) each

Courtesy Locks Gallery, Philadelphia

Kate Moran

Kate Moran's work centers on the human body—often her own, but also surrogates such as dolls and clothing. Her images and objects probe the complexities of growing up female, and the messages they convey are frequently disturbing as they deliberately stretch the accepted norms of feminine representation to explore issues of identity, memory, and social conditioning.

Moran trained in painting and ceramics, and currently works in photography, sculpture, and installations. She moves fluidly between her different mediums, often making interrelated series of works. A group of small figures in cast wax and sewn fabric entitled *nine dolls full of color who understand touch* (checklist 31) provided the subjects for a series of large black-and-white photographs that were originally shown with the dolls in the exhibition *The Grotesque and Ideal* at Lafayette College in Easton, Pennsylvania, in 1995. Sculptures of a pair of shoes, dresses, and leg braces, made in hammered steel with the quality of armor, relate to the stories of the nine dolls and the way in which they address the psychological impact of physiological changes in women.

In her photography Moran extends the conventional boundaries of the medium by applying techniques and materials from other genres. She works her negatives and prints extensively by cutting, sewing, and piercing them—allusions to traditional women's work as well as to surgical procedures and ritual scarification. She has also drawn and painted on some images, and has displayed others surrounded with veils of dyed gauze and dried flowers. These practices result in an aged, fragile quality to her work that underscores the emotional tone of her subjects.

Moran's self-portraits, dolls, and other figures convey a profound sense of vulnerability, as if readily subject to violation, decay, and, ultimately, death. Many of her figures appear physically deformed or suggest states of madness and melancholy. They raise questions about the concept and definition of normalcy by presenting images that lean toward the "abnormal," a concept that Moran values for providing the seeds of "possibility." As she explains, "My themes have focused on challenging ideas of normalcy through transgressive acts. . . . My interest in the grotesque and ideas of excess has to do with the invention of new forms rather than the debasement of forms."[1]

In a series of large photographs from 1993 entitled *Saying and devouring it* (plate 13), Moran uses one of her wax-and-fabric dolls as a prop to enact tableaux of attachment and separation. The images convey a profound ambivalence about the relationship between herself and the doll, raising questions about who controls and who is controlled that allude not only to the human ties but to the artist's struggle to create. In Moran's work the combination of opposites—fragility and strength, pain and pleasure, attraction and repulsion—allows for complex and unsettling reflections such as this on the position and identity of women.

1. Letter to the author, January 20, 1998.

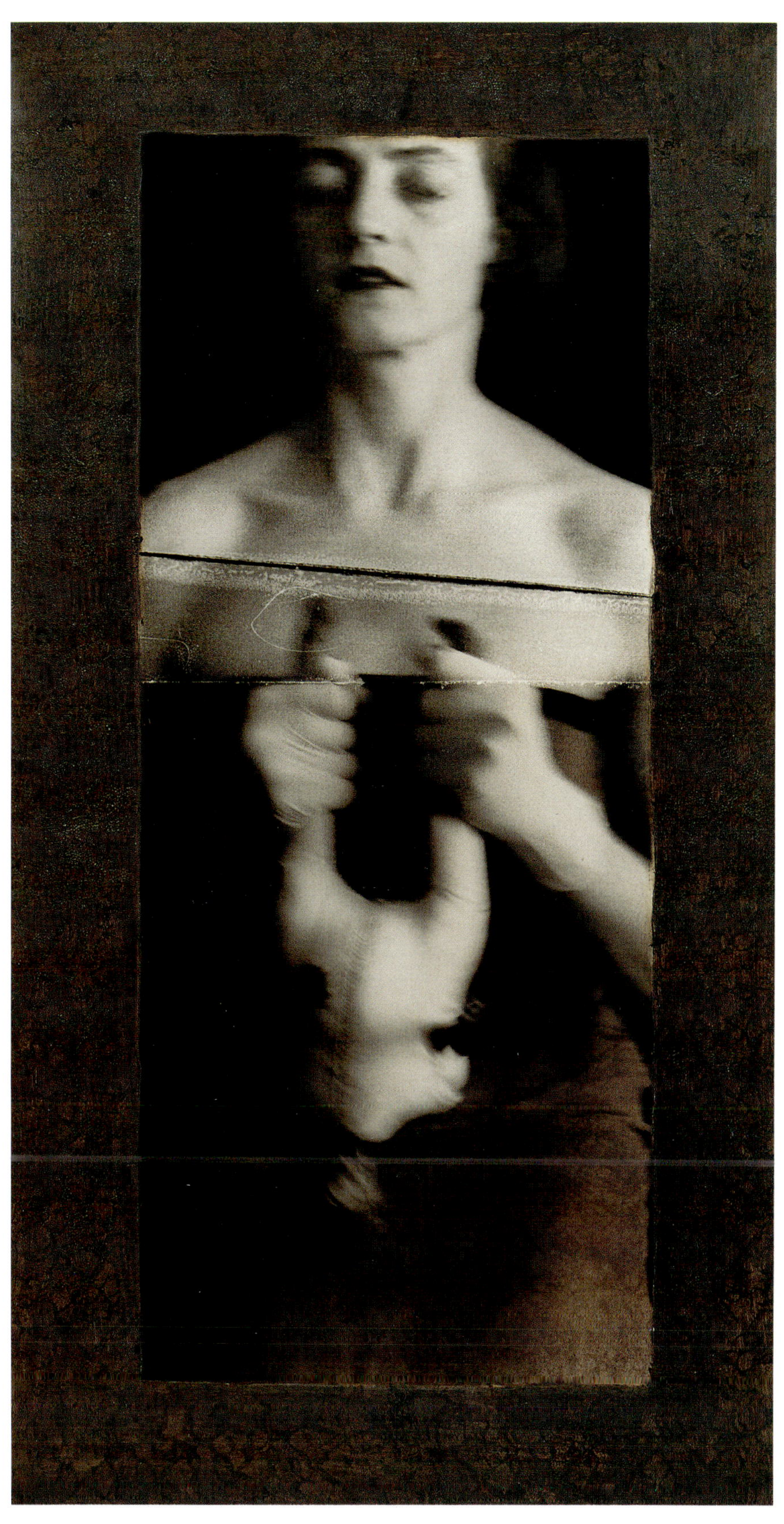

PLATE 13

Kate Moran
Saying and devouring it, 1993
Hand-colored and manipulated
silver print (from a series of three)
48 × 24" (121.9 × 61 cm)
Collection of the artist

Brooke Moyer

Brooke Moyer has said that his sculptures are "about desire and control,"[1] broad concepts that might neatly summarize the motivations of humankind. In Moyer's work they are present on the level of shapes and materials, sources and allusions. His pieces, made of translucent fiberglass and epoxy resin, have an elegant, reductive clarity that resonates with associations to industrial design, plant forms, and the human body, thus contributing their own particular twist to the complex dialogue between nature and culture.

Moyer trained as a ceramicist and only recently began working in epoxy and fiberglass in order to achieve the thin, translucent, and gravity-defying forms that are not possible in clay. His background in clay, however, continues to inform his use of the vessel as a point of departure. His process—in which he casts his materials in molds made from a prototype—also derives from ceramics practice as well as from his training in industrial design.

Although his forms are often based on common, utilitarian objects such as shovels, cleats, and satellite dishes, there is also a strong presence of the body in Moyer's work as well. The seductive surfaces of his sculptures enhance their allusions to animate forms. They have delicate veins of color from drips of tinted resin and a translucent glow as if lit from within, adding to their complex play between inside and outside. They can also convey a sense of something that has been used and discarded, as their brittle shells often surround an emptiness that evokes feelings of sadness and loss.

Each of Moyer's pieces retains a connection to the original function of the object that inspired it while also suggesting new purposes. The flared, mouthlike opening on the perimeter of *Men-an-tol* (plate 14), for example, both invites viewers to look through the ring-shaped body into its center void and transforms a smooth, symmetrical, man-made form into a biological entity.[2] In *More* of 1996 (checklist 33), a giant cone tapers to an aluminum-leafed tip that sports a hole pressed and stamped like an industrial rivet. For Moyer, this detail signals a place where he imagines his piece could be handled and manipulated. By offering a variety of associations—trumpeting flower, oversized industrial funnel, empty cornucopia—whose play between the natural and the manufactured represents "points of connection between our internal desires and external forces,"[3] *More* is full of the humor, irony, and formal elegance that have come to characterize Moyer's work.

1. Artist's statement for his 1997 *Challenge* exhibition, Samuel S. Fleisher Art Memorial, Philadelphia.
2. Moyer explains that *men-an-tol,* which is the name of a Celtic holed stone with various ceremonial purposes, including healing and magic, indicates one of a range of meanings that this shape has held for various cultures. He also mentions his interest in the wall-mounted rings used in a Mayan ball game as an inspiration.
3. Edward J. Sozanski, "Art: Nexus," *Philadelphia Inquirer,* November 22, 1996, Weekend section, p. 40.

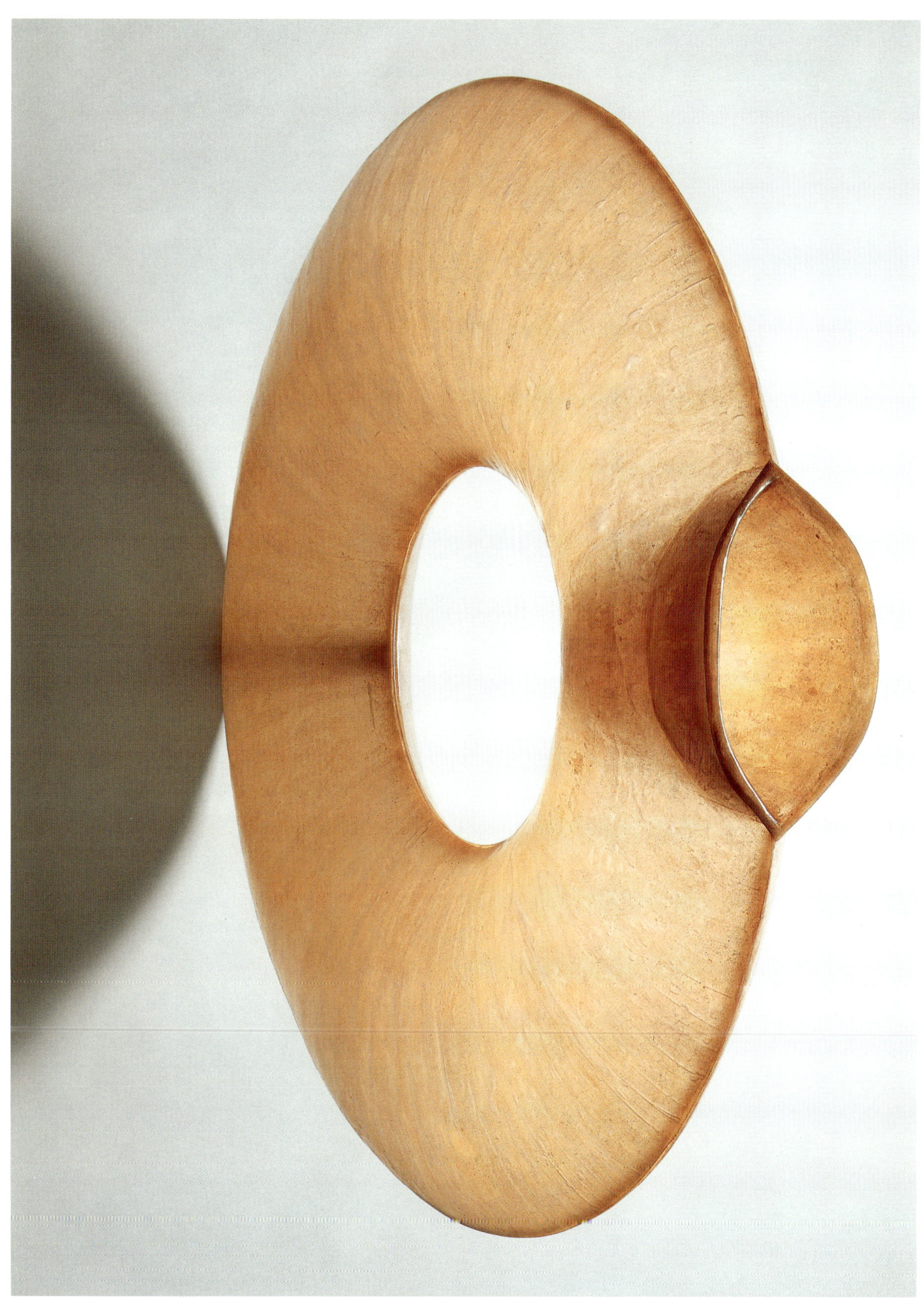

PLATE 14
Brooke Moyer
Men-an-tol, 1996
Epoxy resin, fiberglass, and
pigmented varnish
43 × 44 × 6½" (109.2 × 111.8 × 16.5 cm)
Collection of Douglas Smith

Don Nakamura

Don Nakamura's exuberant, intensely colored ceramic sculpture ranges from precious, hand-size pieces to structures that tower overhead or sprawl across the floor. He hand-builds his work from coils that he covers with a broad array of brightly colored glazes that low-temperature firing allows. His often complex pieces may comprise many stacked, abutted, intertwined, or just proximate units. But even when all their parts are physically joined as one, the works seem born of progressive stages of growth.

Spontaneity and intuition characterize Nakamura's working method. Rather than producing preparatory sketches for his forms, he begins each piece with an idea in his mind's eye, which he modifies as new inspirations arise. As he explains, "Building additively allows for new choices even at the last minute, after the initial concept."[1] Because he works by combining and juxtaposing multiple elements, the drama of his pieces often centers on relationships among the parts (see plate 15). On a basic level, these are relationships between contrasting and complementary forms—linear and spherical, projecting and self-contained, structural and decorative. His use of brightly colored glazes and bold patterns accentuates the similarities and distinctions among the forms, adding a further layer to the animated network of relationships.

Underlying the fantastical, celebratory quality of his objects and assemblages is what Nakamura calls a "deliberate awkwardness." He states that he is "not into precision" in his pieces and "doesn't want the decoration to become too sophisticated." His forms and glazing are reminiscent of a broad range of traditions. Decorative motifs such as multiple eyes, snake forms, abstracted flowers, and geometric patterns draw from archaic, tribal, and folk traditions around the world. His exuberant colors and bulbous, vaguely human forms recall the sculpture of the twentieth-century artists Joan Miró and Niki de Saint-Phalle, including their work in ceramics, while his boldly contrasting approach to pattern builds on the ceramics of Jun Kaneko, with whom Nakamura studied at the Cranbrook Academy of Art.

Nakamura grew up in Hawaii, and the lushness and variety of the islands' natural environment have had a decisive impact on his work. He credits the vibrant colors there, such as the many shades of blue in the water, with inspiring his own use of the full range of available glazes. Tropical plants and flowers also appear as sources of inspiration for fantastical, Dr. Seuss–like hybrid forms. Other pieces have more urban associations, suggesting exuberant, toylike cityscapes, while still others evoke a distinctly human presence. Although Nakamura considers his forms to be abstract translations of experiences, memories, and feelings, he avoids explicit narratives, preferring to leave these allusions open to viewers' interpretations.

1. Conversation with the author, May 27, 1997. All subsequent quotes are from this conversation and one on September 24, 1997.

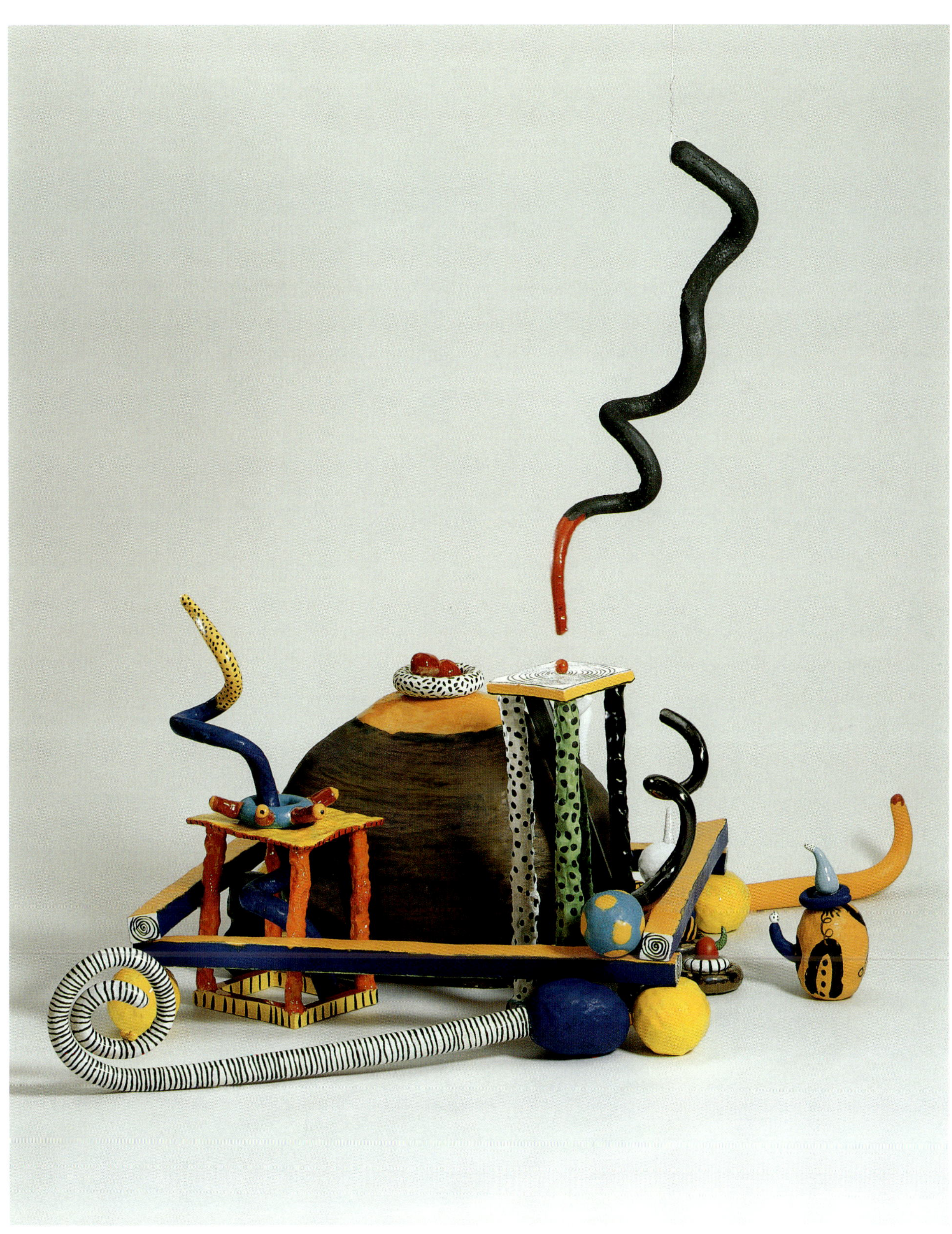

Don Nakamura
My Space, 1996
Low-fire glazes on earthenware and wire
68 × 43 × 75" (172.7 × 109.2 × 190.5 cm)
Collection of the artist

Stuart Netsky

Age-old themes of love, beauty, and the brevity of life animate Stuart Netsky's work, where they are seen from a decidedly contemporary perspective. Using a range of mediums, including painting, sculpture, and photography, he engages the complex intersection of vanity, mortality, and individual identity in ways that hold up traditional values and ideals for reconsideration. He pursues these aims by merging fine art with vernacular culture, often using materials and processes whose associations lie well outside the usual conventions of art.

Netsky has often employed the strategy of appropriation, initiated by artists during the 1980s. His replicas of selected masterpieces of modern painting and sculpture embrace a camp aesthetic famously described by Susan Sontag as the love of "artifice and exaggeration."[1] In a series of works from the late 1980s Netsky built on this strategy of excess. Using billboard flickers—the small, brightly colored plastic discs commonly seen in outdoor commercial advertising—he remade paintings by Claude Monet (see plate 16 and checklist 36), Georges Seurat, Willem de Kooning, Piet Mondrian, and Mark Rothko.[2] These multicolor "flicker paintings," which shimmer with the slightest movement of passersby, stage an unabashed collision of the refined and the vulgar. They are humorous and delicious to behold, but unsettling in their suggestion that our media-saturated eyes and minds must be fed at a level of intensity where the subtlety of past art is superseded by crass appeal.

In another, ongoing body of work using everyday, utilitarian materials, Netsky extends this dialogue of art and artifice. Pouring nail polish down small panels, swirling melted lipstick, and staining stretched linen with hair dye, he has made beautifully crafted, almost precious paintings that serendipitously allude to work by Rothko, Clyfford Still, and Morris Louis. Like his earlier "flicker paintings," these works point to a disjunction between fine art and vernacular culture. But the ease with which cosmetics perform as painting materials also suggests a continuum between making-up a canvas and making-up a face. Netsky owes his proclivity for decoration, domesticity, and fashion in part to his background in studying design at Drexel University and in running a millinery design company in New York before returning to painting and sculpture. But it is also a gutsy embrace of an effeminate stereotype that Netsky transforms from a devalued position to a subversive strategy.[3]

The connection of vanity to mortality that underlies much of Netsky's work comes to the fore in his recastings of classical Greek statuary. One series of plaster sculptures presents Greek gods as aged survivors—Diana with jowls and Venus after a mastectomy—revealing the cruel reality behind the ideal. Another series presents fragments, including Hercules' foot and the ear from Michelangelo's *David*, made using ground-up AIDS drugs combined with binders such as marshmallow and vitamin C. Both these approaches—representing the outward signs of age and decay and incorporating substances intended to fight life-threatening illness—undermine the classical ideals of perfection. They introduce suggestions of death and decay into the realm of the eternal and invincible, following in a tradition of art whose message, *Et in Arcadia ego,* has been understood as "Death exists even in paradise."

1. Susan Sontag, "Notes on 'Camp,'" in Susan Sontag, *Against Interpretation, and Other Essays* (New York, 1990), p. 275.
2. Netsky says he was inspired by billboards for casinos on the highway to Atlantic City and by a sign for a car wash at the corner of Houston Street and Broadway in New York (conversation with the author, October 16, 1997).
3. Bill Arning describes this stereotype as the "decorator/hairstylist/ sissy," and asserts that it is pushed to the margin even within the gay community, where it is seen as an embarrassing anachronism (Arning, "Stuart Netsky: 'Alchemy,'" *Time Out NY,* no. 86 [May 15–22, 1997], p. 46).

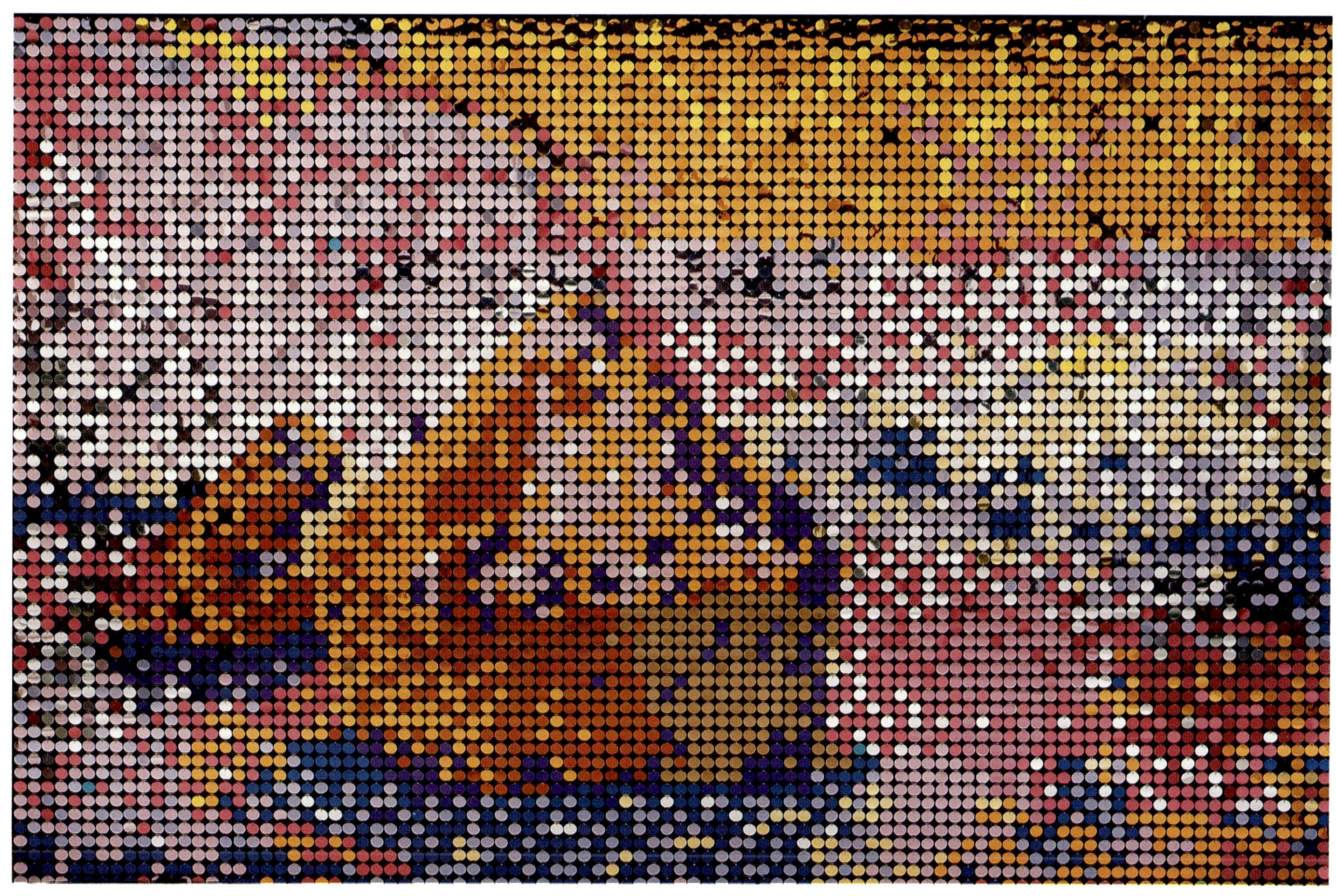

PLATE 16
Stuart Netsky
Monet's Haystacks, 1988
Plastic billboard flickers on
plastic, mounted on wood
78½ × 117½" (199.4 × 298.4 cm)
Collection of the artist, courtesy Larry
Becker Contemporary Art, Philadelphia

Bruce Pollock

Abstract forms and patterns, most often derived from nature, provide the source for Bruce Pollock's meditative, complex paintings. These are images of meandering lines, concentric and spiraling matrices, radiating and branching forms, and crystalline structures. They spread across the surfaces of his works in allover dispersals recalling the color-field painting that still dominated the art schools when Pollock studied in the mid-1970s. Although his forms have an organic quality, his interest is not in replicating the natural structures he favors, but in using them as points of departure to create areas of activity that in turn suggest their own forms.

Not all of Pollock's sources are found in nature, however. In the late 1970s and early 1980s, he was producing small, painted structures that derived from such architectural sources as Philadelphia's row houses, which the artist admired for their endless variety.[1] Common regional buildings discovered during back-road country drives also inspired this body of work, as did the architectural photographs of Walker Evans, and the notions about vernacular architecture of the Philadelphia firm of Robert Venturi and Denise Scott Brown.[2]

Pollock built his painted house forms with wood from fruit crates found in Philadelphia's Italian Market (see checklist 41–45). He slowly covered their surfaces with many layers of enamel paints in discontinued colors that he bought at a discount. He sanded down the built-up surfaces, unevenly removing paint to reveal the many underlayers and the grain of the wood. Pollock imagined these structures as seashell-like, formed by a time-consuming process of accretion and abrasion. Although the houses owe their simple geometry and placement directly on the floor to the Minimalist sculpture of the 1960s, their capacity to evoke a range of associations, compounded by their toylike presence, lends them a nostalgic quality that is further enhanced by their weathered surfaces.

If these early pieces felt like painted sculpture, the work that followed in the mid-1980s could be seen as sculpted paintings whose surfaces were built up and sanded back down using a similar combination of additive and subtractive processes. At first still using enamel paint, Pollock worked on panels as long as eight feet that he imagined as the enlarged insides of the houses. In his subsequent work, he abandoned enamel paint and the sanding process with their toxic dangers, building up relief surfaces with acrylics instead. Since 1990, Pollock has painted almost exclusively in oil on canvas as he has moved away from the emphasis on labor-intensive handwork that evokes the passage of time.

The diversity of Pollock's work is united by the concept of change. His recent paintings—complex layerings of patterns and forms—present images of gradually but continuously shifting relationships between figure and ground (see plate 17). They have a playful humor, a gamelike quality in which various elements might suddenly appear to change, creating a whole new configuration. As Pollock has explained, "When you look at nature it doesn't reveal itself immediately. The more you look, the more that you see. . . . It just keeps opening up in different ways. I work hard at trying to make a painting do that."[3] These are images of transformation—"fields of energy," as the artist refers to them. They reward prolonged looking with a slow unraveling of their secrets and with the sense that through them one is contemplating larger issues of creation and existence.

1. Approximately fifty of these were displayed on the floor in his 1979 *Challenge* exhibition, Samuel S. Fleisher Art Memorial, Philadelphia.
2. At that time, Pollock's studio was next to Venturi and Scott Brown's center-city office.
3. Conversation with the author, April 8, 1997. The subsequent quote is from the same conversation.

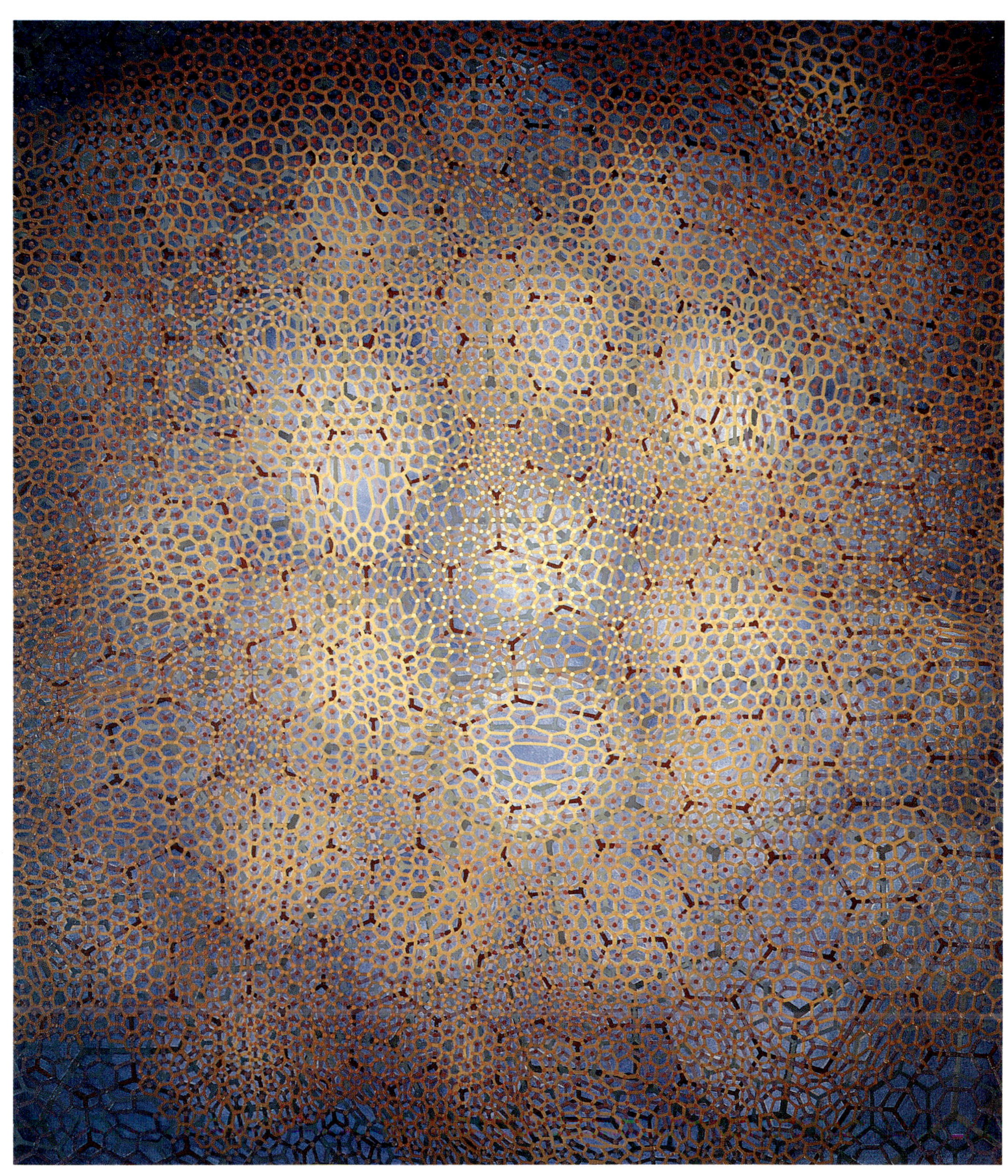

PLATE 17
Bruce Pollock
Net of Indra, 1997
Oil on canvas
70 × 60" (177.8 × 152.4 cm)
Courtesy Fleisher/Ollman Gallery,
Philadelphia

Judith Schaechter

Judith Schaechter's work in stained glass presents a panoply of sin, disaster, violence, and distress in a medium capable of transcendent beauty. Schaechter welcomes her chosen medium's strong associations with its traditional function of conveying Christian theology in churches and cathedrals across the Western world. In the late nineteenth century, Louis Comfort Tiffany's technical innovations expanded its use into domestic and other secular settings. Schaechter has looked to both traditions for inspiration in developing her unique approach to stained glass, which combines the spiritual appeal of colored light with a gruesome and melancholy subject matter that is at once timeless and thoroughly contemporary.

The basic drives of life—love and hate, sex and fear, pleasure and pain—are the focus of Schaechter's work. These are the themes of countless ancient tales as well as the stuff of tabloids, television, and everyday life, and Schaechter puts the seductive beauty of her medium to full use in telling her compelling stories. Her protagonists are mostly young women with sad, weary expressions who follow in a venerable tradition of sorrowfully stoic martyrs. Through natural disasters and physical illness, failed crimes and futile rescues, sex, violence, and death, Schaechter's figures are presented with sympathy—not with approval exactly, but with a tenderness that suggests her appreciation for their suffering. These are morality tales, but without the moralizing.

Until the late 1980s Schaechter's work had a brutal directness based on simply modeled figures presented alone in shallow, confining spaces. Around the time of her Fleisher *Challenge* show in 1990, she abandoned the age-old method of joining the separate pieces of glass with thick channels of lead in favor of the copper foil technique invented by Tiffany. Now she could place two or more panes of glass flush together with no gap in between, allowing a much greater range of tonalities. Using flash glass—clear sheets of glass with veneers of color that she selectively removes by scratching, etching, or sandblasting—she has developed the ability to truly model flesh in glass. Simultaneously her drawing of figures and their surrounding spaces became more sophisticated, furthering her move toward increasingly elaborate compositions and narratives (see plate 18).

Schaechter has described her approach to art as "taking ugly things and making them beautiful."[1] In this way she places herself in an anticlassical tradition that runs from Gothic art through German Expressionism and contemporary underground culture, one that depicts the human body as a vessel for powerful internal and external forces that distort its outward appearance. Ultimately Schaechter's jewel-like work is a potent mixture of opposites, where beauty and tragedy, seduction and repulsion, fuel each other, and ecstasy is nearly indistinguishable from pain.

1. Quoted in A. B. Roberto, "Quick Sketch: Portrait of the Artist as Medievalist," *Art Matters,* June 1997, p. 12.

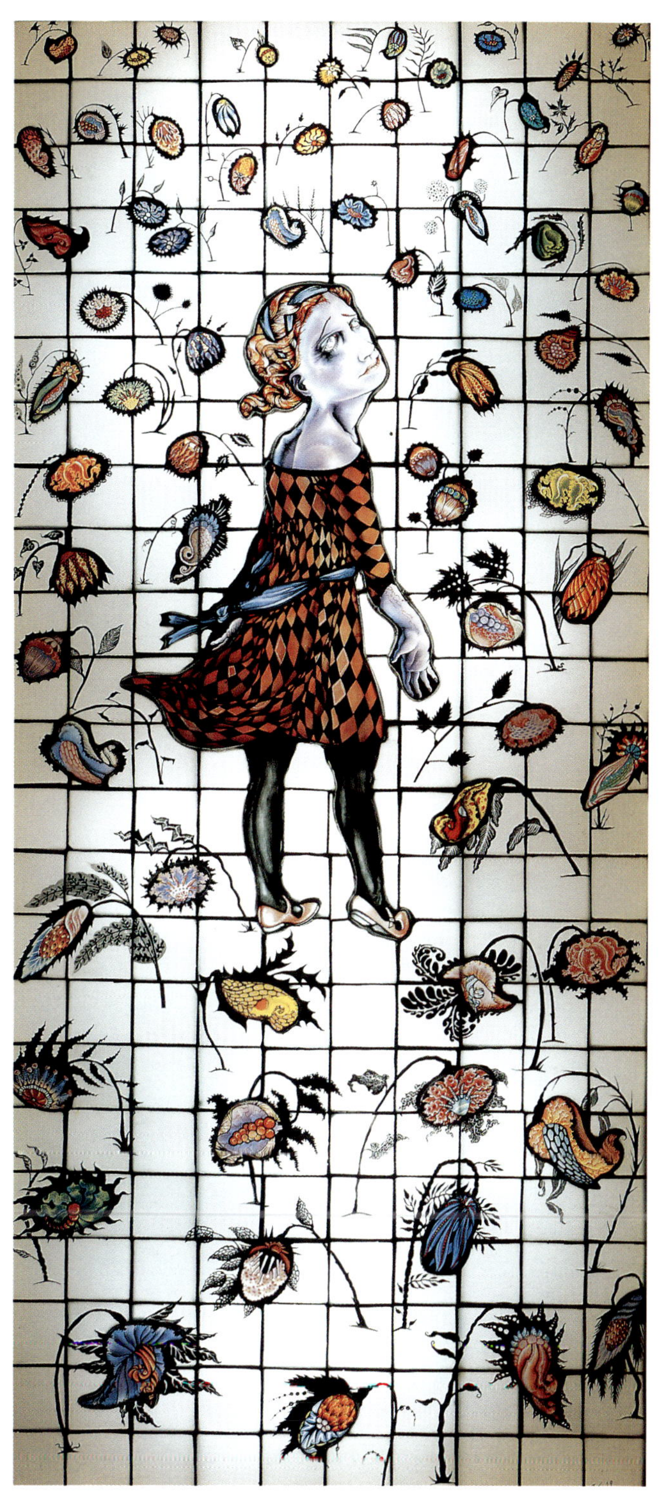

Judith Schaechter
I've Trampled a Million Pretty Flowers, 1995
Stained glass
47 × 21" (119.4 × 53.3 cm)
Philadelphia Museum of Art. Gift of
the Women's Committee of the
Philadelphia Museum of Art. 1995-81-2

Hester Stinnett

Over the two decades of Hester Stinnett's printmaking career, her work has evolved from elaborately carved black-and-white woodblock prints of imagined landscapes to abstract, experimental monoprints. In her work from the early 1980s, she invented scenes of fields and forests, inspired by memories of her grandfather's loblolly pine tree farm in Louisiana.[1] In 1987, however, Stinnett began to move away from representational imagery. She started making monotypes (each a unique print) by inking wooden planks, some carved or gouged, others left untouched, and printing them by rubbing with her hands or with spoons and other tools to create irregular imprints. With their prominent wood grain and narrow, vertical plank forms, these austere, architectonic images retained a connection to her earlier tree imagery. But in these improvisational works Stinnett had made the crucial step from depicting an object to printing directly from it.

Over time, Stinnett became aware that she was relying on repeated devices to resolve her compositions. She wanted to retain the act-and-react method that had underpinned this series, while still finding a way to subvert her imposed control. Stinnett's studies of John Cage's work, in particular his incorporation of chance as a creative strategy, provided a key to this process. Around the same time, in 1991, Stinnett discovered *suminagashi,* an ancient Japanese technique for marbling paper by dipping a sheet into water to pick up the ink floating on the surface. Because the pattern of the ink is highly sensitive to such environmental variables as temperature, vibrations, and humidity, the paper captures an unpredictable moment as it hits the water, thus making a permanent record of a dynamic process.

Stinnett used little or no intervention in her early *suminagashi* prints, which suggest natural processes of growth such as cell division or tree rings. As her working method evolved, she began to insert woodblock-printed images, whose deliberate, manufactured character created a dialogue with the organic *suminagashi* images, thus making evident the interplay between chance and decision. Subsequently, Stinnett started to explore how her interventions and the unpredictable *suminagashi* could occur simultaneously rather than sequentially. She would first print images on paper in clear varnish, whose invisible presence would be revealed by the *suminagashi* process, a convergence out of the artist's control.

For her printed imagery, Stinnett first used organizational structures—including a computer map of the Andromeda galaxy and an old chart from her father's school showing the flow of students between rooms—and photograms of string and twigs. More recently, she has printed snippets of handwriting made by her mother as she suffered through dementia (see plate 19). A meticulous note writer and recordkeeper, her mother continued this practice throughout her decline as she struggled to maintain control over a radically changing situation. Within a note or even a single word, her handwriting would change from clarity to total confusion. Stinnett understood these notes as being parallel to the dynamic she was seeking in her printmaking. This was underscored by the knowledge that when *suminagashi* was invented in the twelfth century, poets and calligraphers used its appearance of spontaneity as inspiration for verses on changes in everyday life and the passage of time that they wrote upon the printed sheets. Stinnett imagines her use of her mother's notes (and those of a family friend) as a similar collaboration between chance and control.

1. Letter to the author, September 9, 1997.

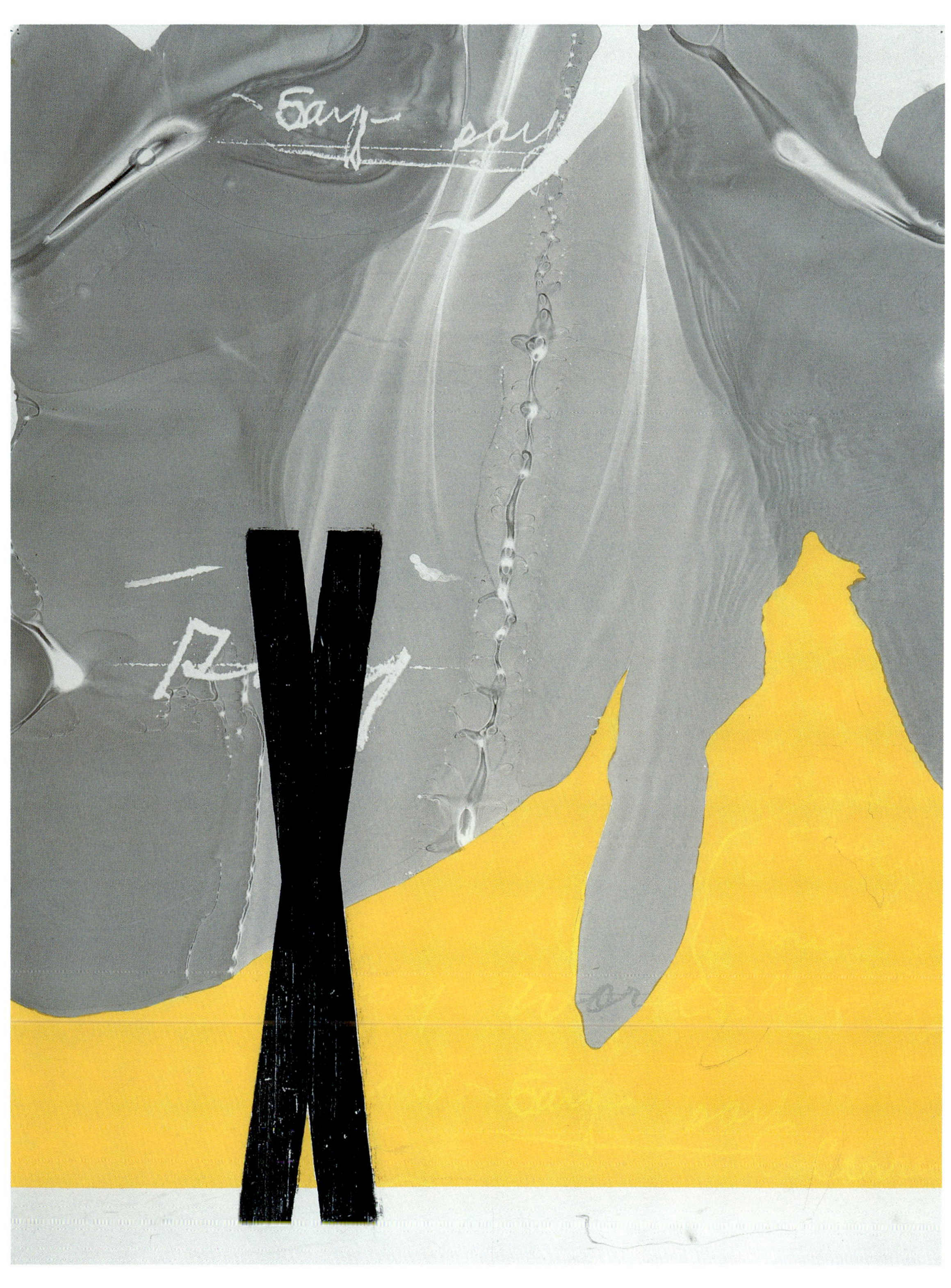

Hester Stinnett

#127, 1997
Suminagashi, woodblock, and screen print
36 × 27" (91.4 × 68.6 cm)
Collection of the artist

Stephen Talasnik

The subject that unites twenty years of Stephen Talasnik's drawings is time, time made manifest by structure, form, and process. His early images were inspired by everyday objects, some found in abandoned buildings, which he altered to appear as ritual or mummified artifacts. In more recent works Talasnik pushes structural forms—architecture, industrial complexes, urban planning maps, construction sites, airplane wing design, and joinery—beyond descriptive rendering. His interest is in developing narrative and symbolic functions, which leads him to mutate, degrade, combine, and recontextualize his sources in ways that build on the capacity of manmade objects and structures to evoke different periods of time, real or imagined.

Seeing the landmark *Drawing Now* exhibition at the Museum of Modern Art in New York in 1976 while he was a graduate student confirmed Talasnik's early ambition to make drawing an end in itself rather than a means to serve other mediums. His year in Rome in 1977–78 while a graduate student at the Tyler School of Art was pivotal for developing his interest in history, archaeology, and architecture as primary subjects. His subsequent travels, including three years in Japan (1987–90), reinforced his understanding of the physical environments of different cities—their structures and infrastructures—as embodying different moments in time and allowing for a sense of connection with the past generations who used and inhabited them. Other forms that have inspired ongoing series of drawings include fossils and shrouds,[1] two other means by which imprints of the past can be conveyed to the present.

In his early work Talasnik used pencil and charcoal to create glowing light and deep shadows evocative of old photography. Over the last decade, however, he has developed a drawing process that more directly embodies the passage of time. Working exclusively with graphite on paper in a process that is both additive and subtractive, he draws, erases, and redraws; abrades the paper with sandpaper, steel wool, and wire brushes; and adds images by making rubbings from woodblocks that create frottage elements with an altogether different quality than wholly invented marks. The multilayered appearance of his images contain ample evidence of labor as the measure of time's passing. They also suggest the effects of weathering and decay by natural forces. Memory, too—as the place where the passage of time is recorded, ordered, shuffled, and reexperienced—underlies these powerful works.

Talasnik refers to his recent work as "visionary objects," a term he enjoys for its allusion to the visionary architecture of the French Neoclassical architects Claude-Nicolas Ledoux and Etienne-Louis Boullée, whose fantastic utopian projects are known primarily through their drawings. In Talasnik's recent works, he has eliminated the dark grounds and hazy atmospheres that surrounded his earlier images, removing the vestiges of associations to photography and printmaking. These tend to be single, iconic forms, networks of skeletal structure in more open environments that allow them a fluidity of scale—alternately intimate and monumental (see plate 20). Talasnik understands the capacity of drawing to stimulate the imagination with incomplete, obscured, and densely layered imagery. Through his original and sophisticated manipulations of the drawing medium, he gives his ostensibly rational forms a patina of the irrational, putting them in the service of fantasy rather than reason.

1. Talasnik's specific source of inspiration is the Shroud of Turin, which is believed to bear an imprint of Christ's body.

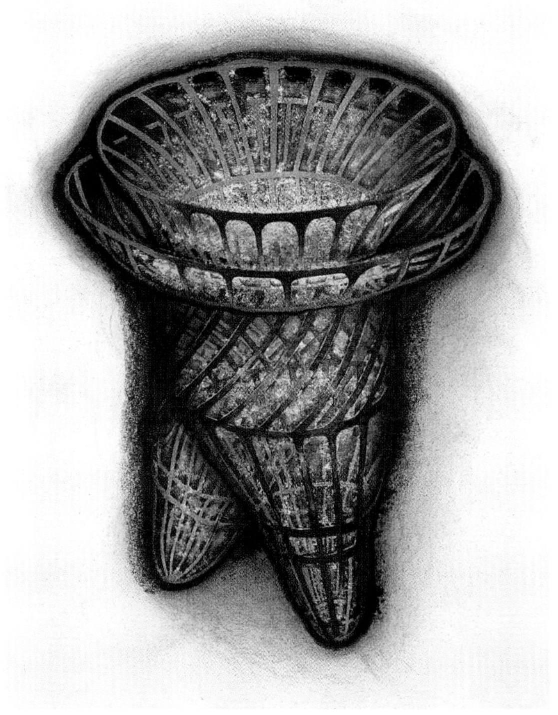
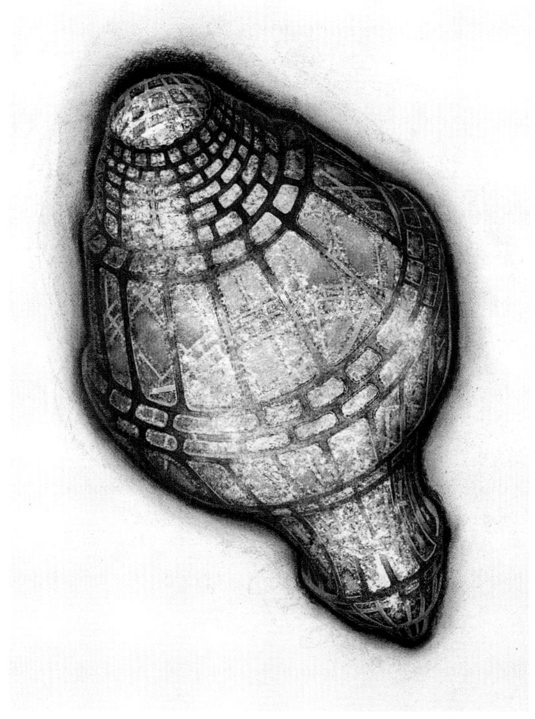
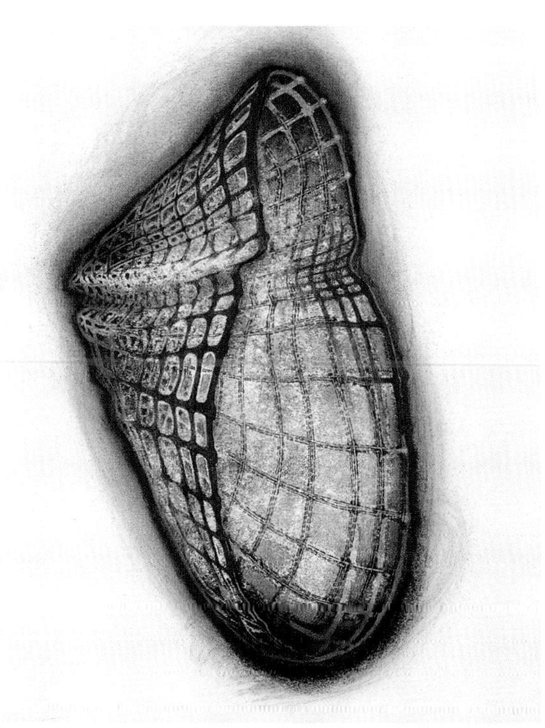
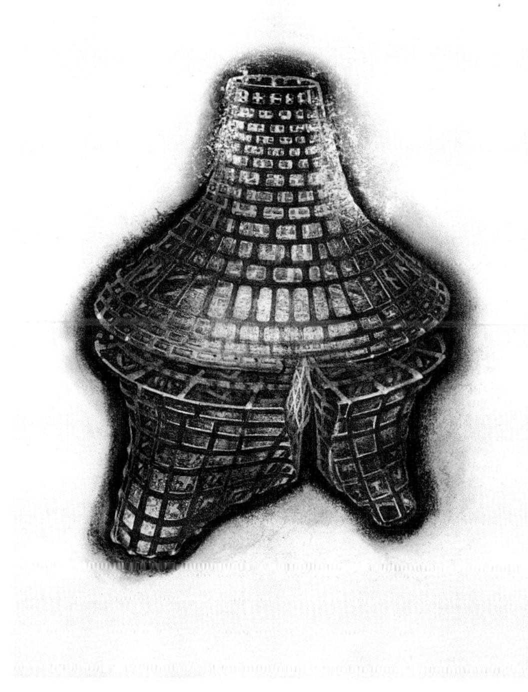

Stephen Talasnik
Visionary Objects: Implant, Beacon, Split,
and *Pinch* (clockwise from upper left), 1997
Graphite on paper
22 × 17" (55.9 × 43.2 cm) each
Collection of the artist (*Implant, Beacon, Pinch*)
Collection of Sydnee and Seymour Martin Lipset (*Split*)

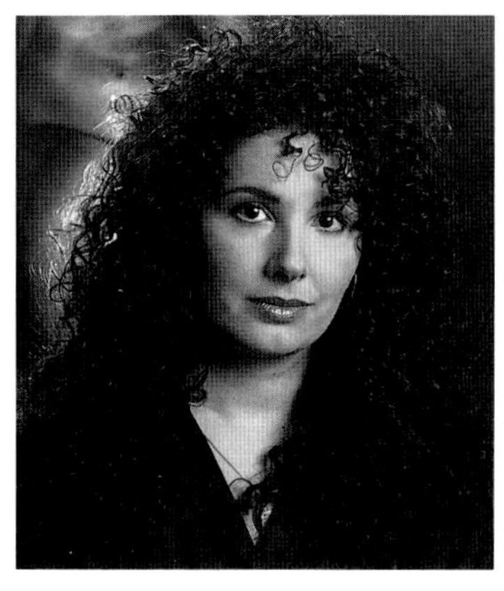

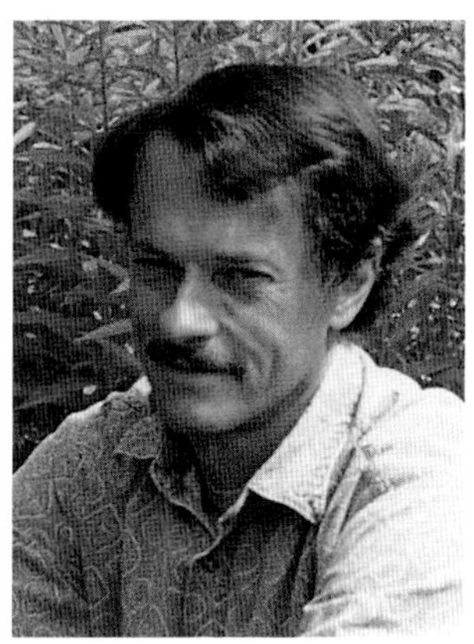

Lisa Bartolozzi

Born
1961 Baltimore

Studied
1989 M.F.A. in painting, School of Fine
Arts, Washington University, Saint Louis
1984 B.F.A. in painting, University of
Delaware, Newark

Teaches Horizons, The New England Craft
Program, Sunderland, Massachusetts

Resides Newark, Delaware

***Challenge* exhibition** 1994

Selected solo exhibitions
1997 *Recent Paintings and Drawings,*
Delaware Art Museum, Wilmington
1992 *Recent Work,* Delaware State Arts
Council, Carvel State Building, Wilmington
1987 *Paintings and Drawings,* Delaware
State Arts Council, Carvel State Building,
Wilmington

Selected group exhibitions
1997 *The Derriere Guard Festival,* The
Kitchen, New York
1996 *Syne: Beyond Language,* Downtown
Art Gallery, Delaware Art Museum,
Wilmington; Watford Museum, England
1994 *Italian-American Women Artists,*
Florence-Philadelphia; Galleria della Nuova
Stazione Statuo, Florence
1992 *Figures of Eight: Painters of the Human
Form,* Delaware Center for the Contem-
porary Arts, Wilmington

Lanny Bergner

Born
1952 Anacortes, Washington

Studied
1983 M.F.A. in sculpture, Tyler School of
Art, Temple University, Philadelphia
1981 B.F.A. in sculpture, University of
Washington, Seattle

Resides Anacortes, Washington

***Challenge* exhibition** 1984

Selected solo exhibitions
1996 *Recent Sculpture,* Foundation Gallery,
Skagit Valley College, Mount Vernon,
Washington
　Sculpture, Allied Arts of Whatcom
County, Bellingham, Washington
　Sculpture, Commencement Art Gallery,
Tacoma Arts Commission, Washington
1993 *Sculpture,* Gallery K, Washington, D.C.
1992 *Aberrations,* Locks Gallery, Phila-
delphia
1990 *Earth Bound,* Marian Locks Gallery,
Philadelphia
1988 *Sculpture,* Gallery K, Washington, D.C.
　Un/Natural, Swarthmore College,
Pennsylvania

Selected group exhibitions
1996 *Recent Acquisitions,* Seattle Art
Museum
1995 *Fiber '95,* Textiles Art Center, Chicago
1994 *Rutgers National '94: Works on Paper,*
Stedman Art Gallery, Rutgers University,
Camden, New Jersey

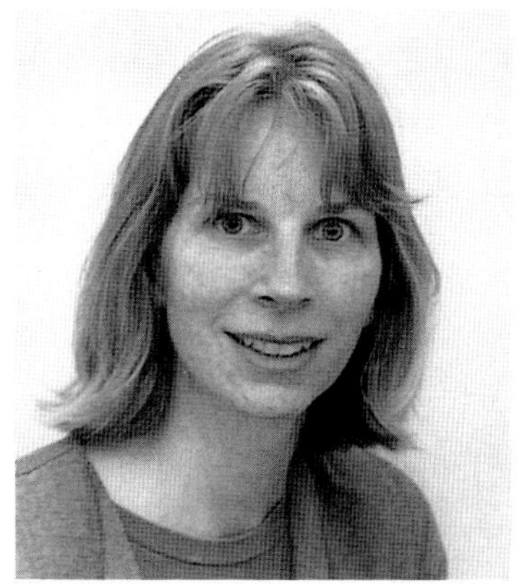

Norinne Betjemann

1993 *Lanny Bergner/Frank Galuszka: Recent Work,* Morris Gallery, Pennsylvania Academy of the Fine Arts, Philadelphia
1991 *Biennial '91,* Delaware Art Museum, Wilmington
Philadelphia Art Now: Artists Choose Artists, Institute of Contemporary Art, Philadelphia
1990 *Contemporary Philadelphia Artists: A Juried Exhibition,* Philadelphia Museum of Art
1989 *Landscapes of Thought,* Momenta Art Alternatives, Philadelphia
1988 *Altered Sites,* Horticultural Center, Fairmount Park, Philadelphia
Natural Transformations, Art in General, New York
1987 *Four Contemporary Artists,* Allentown Art Museum, Pennsylvania

Born
1959 Princeton, New Jersey

Studied
1997 M.A. in education, Goldsmiths College, University of London
1995 Postgraduate diploma in arts administration and teaching, Birkbeck College, University of London
1981 B.F.A. in photography, Moore College of Art and Design, Philadelphia

Resides London

Challenge exhibition 1989

Selected solo exhibitions
1995 *Breathing in Irrespirable Atmosphere,* Sande Webster Gallery, Philadelphia
1994 Figure 5 Gallery, San Francisco
1993 *Architektonische Photographie,* Michel Hensel/Kunstraum am Buttermarkt, Cologne, Germany
1992 *An Ahistorical Past,* Virginia Foundation for Architecture, Richmond; The Williamsburg Center for the Arts, Virginia
1991 *Architectural Photographs,* American Institute of Architects National Headquarters Gallery, Washington, D.C.
Land of Infancy, Dennis Hotz Fine Arts Limited, London

1990 *Endroits non définis (Areas Non-defined),* Espace A.G.F., Paris
Flood, Jessica Berwind Gallery and The Print Club, Philadelphia
1988 *In Time,* Red Column Studio, Philadelphia

Selected group exhibitions
1993 *Present Remains,* Art in General, New York
Three Photographers, Delaware Art Museum, Wilmington
1990 *Contemporary Philadelphia Artists: A Juried Exhibition,* Philadelphia Museum of Art
Selections from the Graham and Susan Nash Collection, Los Angeles County Museum of Art
Through Another's Eye, Delaware Art Museum, Wilmington
1989 *Biennial '89,* Delaware Art Museum, Wilmington
Surface Appearances: The Painted Photograph, John Michael Kohler Arts Center, Sheboygan, Wisconsin

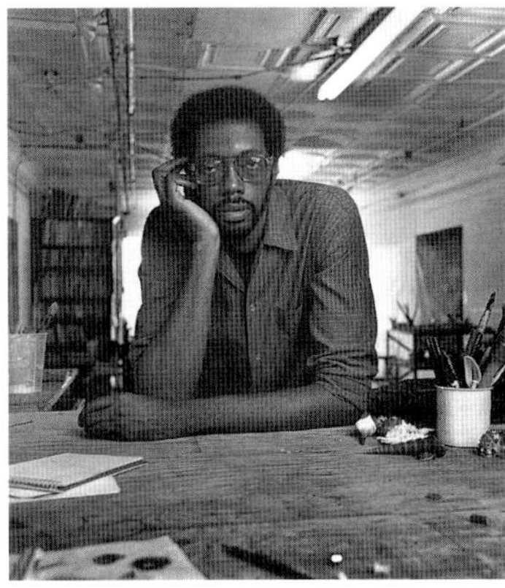

Charles Burwell

Born
1955 Henderson, North Carolina

Studied
1979 M.F.A. in painting, Yale University, New Haven, Connecticut
1977 B.F.A. in painting, Tyler School of Art, Temple University, Philadelphia

Resides Philadelphia

***Challenge* exhibition** 1985

Selected solo exhibitions
1997 Sande Webster Gallery, Philadelphia
1995 *Paintings and Drawings,* Jaffe-Friede and Strauss Galleries, Hopkins Center, Dartmouth College, Hanover, New Hampshire
1994 Sande Webster Gallery, Philadelphia
1992 *Paintings and Drawings,* Sherry Washington Gallery, Detroit
   Recent Work, Second Street Gallery, Charlottesville, Virginia
1991 *New Directions,* Sande Webster Gallery, Philadelphia
1990 *Paintings,* Susan Isaacs Gallery, Wilmington; Hudson D. Walker Gallery at the Fine Arts Work Center, Provincetown, Massachusetts
1989 Sherry Washington Gallery, Detroit
1980 Downtown Art Gallery, Delaware Art Museum, Wilmington

Selected group exhibitions
1996 *Biennial '96,* Delaware Art Museum, Wilmington
   Creative Artists Network: Selections, 1984–96, Woodmere Art Museum, Philadelphia
   55th Annual Awards Painting Exhibition, Cheltenham Center for the Arts
1994 *Artists Select,* Artist's Space, New York
1993 *Hard Choices III: Pennsylvania Council on the Arts, Visual Arts Fellowship Recipients Exhibition,* Southern Alleghenies Museum of Art at Johnstown, Pennsylvania
   Rutgers Center for Innovative Printmaking: Fellowship Recipients, Mason Gross School of the Arts, Rutgers University, New Brunswick, New Jersey
1992 *African American Artists in the Twentieth Century: The Philadelphia Connection,* Philadelphia Art Alliance
1991 *Recherche: Transpired Realities,* Afro-American Historical and Cultural Museum, Philadelphia
1988 *Treasures from the Permanent Collection, 1970–87,* The Studio Museum in Harlem, New York
1984 Art in General Gallery, New York
1980 *Expressions '80,* Afro-American Historical and Cultural Museum, Philadelphia

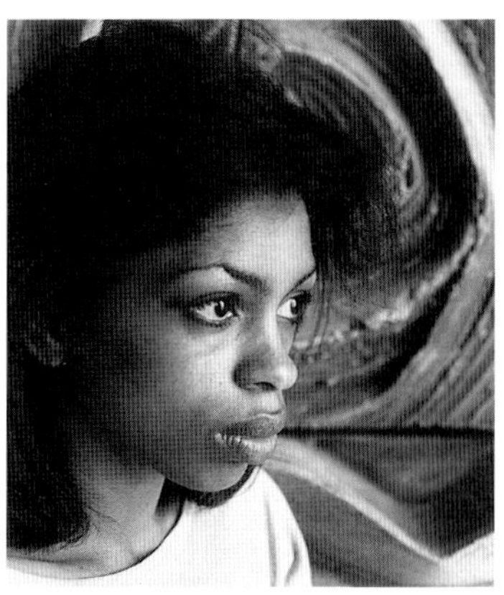

Syd Carpenter

Born
1953 Pittsburgh

Studied
1976 M.F.A. in ceramics, Tyler School of Art, Temple University, Philadelphia
1974 B.F.A. in painting and ceramics, Tyler School of Art, Temple University, Philadelphia

Teaches Swarthmore College, Pennsylvania

Resides Philadelphia

***Challenge* exhibition** 1989

Selected solo exhibitions
1997 *Bound,* Sande Webster Gallery, Philadelphia
1994 Sande Webster Gallery, Philadelphia
1985 *Wallpieces and Containers,* Sande Webster Gallery, Philadelphia

Selected group exhibitions
1997 *Syd Carpenter/Michael Lucero,* Northern Clay Center, Saint Paul, Minnesota
   Women Mentoring Women, Westby Art Gallery, Rowan University, Glassboro, New Jersey
1995 *Contained/Uncontained,* Dallas Museum of African American Art

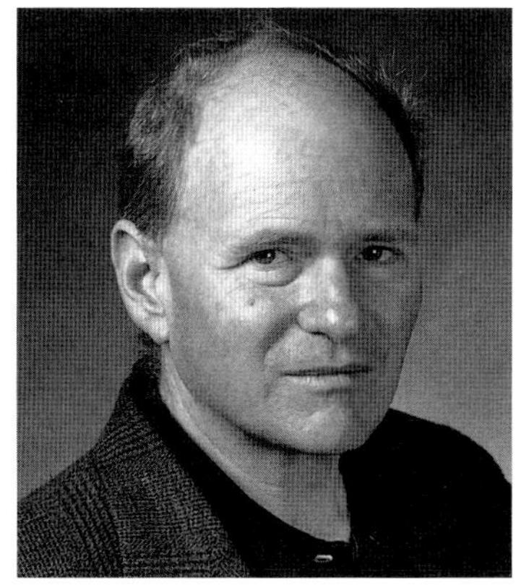

Frank Galuszka

Born
1947 Newark, New Jersey

Studied
1972 M.F.A. in painting, Tyler School of Art, Temple University, Rome
1969 B.F.A. in painting, Tyler School of Art, Temple University, Philadelphia

Teaches University of California, Santa Cruz

Resides Santa Cruz, California

***Challenge* exhibition** 1978

Selected solo exhibitions
1997 *Kali and Venus*, The More Gallery, Philadelphia
1996 *Paintings,* Revolution, Ferndale, Michigan
1995 The More Gallery, Philadelphia
1993 The More Gallery, Philadelphia
1990 *From About Then*, University of the Arts, Philadelphia
1989 The More Gallery, Philadelphia
1988 Nicholas Roerich Museum, New York
1987 The More Gallery, Philadelphia
1986 *Blue Paintings*, Seton Hall University, South Orange, New Jersey
1984 The More Gallery, Philadelphia
1982 Butcher and More Galleries, Philadelphia
1977 New England College, Henniker, New Hampshire
1976 Stockton State College, Pomona, New Jersey

1993 *Clay National*, Everson Museum of Art, Syracuse, New York
1992 *Clay Heritage: African American Ceramics*, Afro-American Historical and Cultural Museum, Philadelphia
1989 *Spirit Within*, Henry Street Settlement, New York
1983 *The Soup Tureen Show*, Campbell Museum, Camden, New Jersey

1976 Hahn Gallery, Philadelphia
1975 Cheltenham Center for the Arts

Selected group exhibitions
1996 *A Chaos of Delight: Artists and Scientists Seek an Understanding of Their World*, Delaware Center for the Contemporary Arts, Wilmington
1993 *Lanny Bergner/Frank Galuszka: Recent Work*, Morris Gallery, Pennsylvania Academy of the Fine Arts, Philadelphia
 The Return of "Cadavre Exquis," Drawing Center, New York
1990 *Contemporary Philadelphia Art: A Juried Exhibition*, Philadelphia Museum of Art
1986 *161st Annual Exhibition*, National Academy of Design, New York

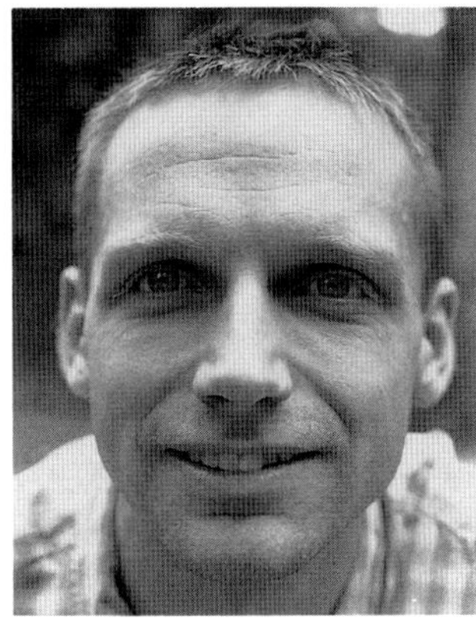

Michael Grothusen

Born
1966 Holden, Missouri

Studied
1991 M.F.A. in sculpture, Tyler School of
Art, Temple University, Philadelphia
   Skowhegan School of Painting and
Sculpture, Maine
1988 B.F.A. in sculpture, University of
Kansas, Lawrence
1986–87 Brighton Polytechnic, England

Teaches Drexel University, Philadelphia
   Tyler School of Art, Temple University,
Philadelphia
      University of the Arts, Philadelphia

Resides Philadelphia

Challenge **exhibition** 1992

Selected solo exhibitions
1998 *Be Here Now*, Hewlett Gallery,
College of Fine Arts, Carnegie Mellon
University, Pittsburgh
1997 *Ordinary Sculpture,* Gallery Joe,
Philadelphia
   Residue, Philadelphia Art Alliance
   Window on Broad, University of the Arts,
Philadelphia

Selected group exhibitions
1997 *Construction Site*, Levy Gallery for the
Arts in Philadelphia, Moore College of Art
and Design
   Objects and Souvenirs: Artist's Multiples,
Rosenwald-Wolf Gallery, University of the
Arts, Philadelphia
1996 *25th Annual Juried Show*, Allentown
Art Museum, Pennsylvania
1995 *Six Sculptors*, Long Island University,
Brookville, New York
1994 *Garden Matrix*, Abington Art Center,
Jenkintown, Pennsylvania
1993 *Recovering the Landscape,* Chester
Springs Studio, Pennsylvania
1991 *Biennial '91,* Delaware Art Museum,
Wilmington

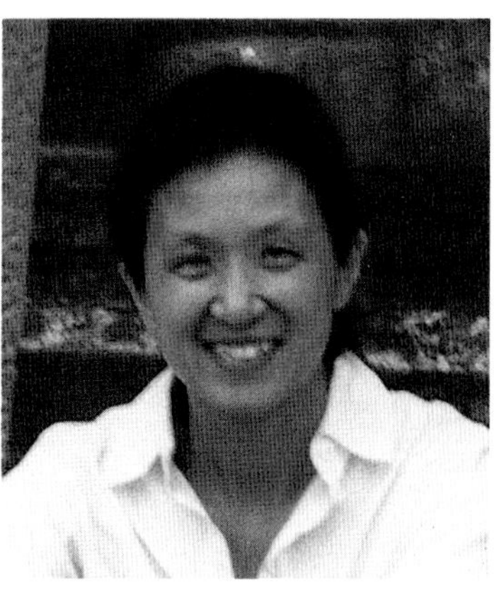

Mei-ling Hom

Born
1951 New Haven, Connecticut

Studied
1987 M.F.A. in sculpture, New York State
College of Ceramics at Alfred University,
Alfred, New York
1973 B.A. in sculpture, Kirkland College,
Clinton, New York

Teaches Community College of
Philadelphia

Resides Philadelphia

Challenge **exhibition** 1991

Selected solo exhibitions
1996 *Offering*, The Alternative Museum,
New York
1994 *Photography and Community*, Asian
American Arts Center, New York
   *Picturing Asian America: A Community
Collaboration*, Levy Gallery for the Arts in
Philadelphia, Moore College of Art and
Design
1993 *Thai Space*, Faculty of Sculpture,
Painting, and Graphic Arts Gallery,
Silpakorn University, Bangkok, Thailand
1990 *944 Barracks*, The Headlands Center
for the Arts, Sausalito, California
1985 *Architectural Clay/Clay in Architecture*,
Jane Hartsook Gallery, New York
1984 Marian Locks Gallery East,
Philadelphia
1983 Quinnipiac State College, Hamden,
Connecticut
1980 Marian Locks Gallery, Philadelphia

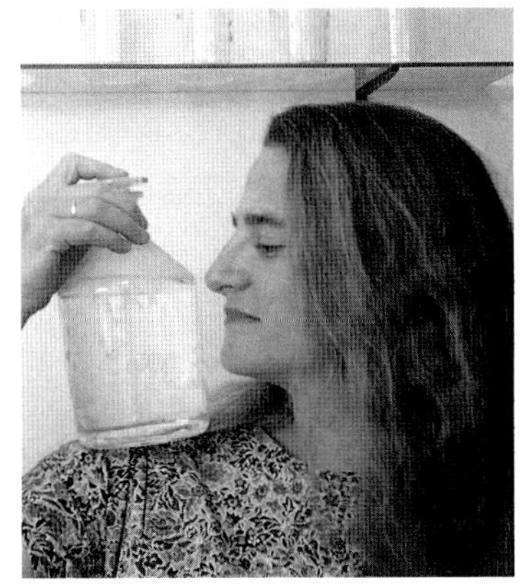

Stacy Levy

Selected commissions
1994 *China Wedge,* Pennsylvania Convention Center, Philadelphia

Selected group exhibitions
1996 *Nature Morte: Contemporary Still Life,* Museum of American Art, Pennsylvania Academy of the Fine Arts, Philadelphia
1994 *Guardians of the Earth,* Rosemont College, Pennsylvania
1991 *Artists Choose Artists,* Institute of Contemporary Art, Philadelphia
The Asian Experience in Philadelphia, Painted Bride Art Center, Philadelphia
Biennial '91, Delaware Art Museum, Wilmington
1990 *Contemporary Philadelphia Artists: A Juried Exhibition,* Philadelphia Museum of Art
Perspectives from Pennsylvania, Temporal Sculpture: Site Works, Carnegie Mellon Art Gallery, Pittsburgh
1988 *Altered Sites,* Horticultural Center, Fairmount Park, Philadelphia

Born
1960 Philadelphia

Studied
1991 M.F.A. in sculpture, Tyler School of Art, Temple University, Philadelphia
1988 Skowhegan School of Painting and Sculpture, Maine
1984 B.A. in sculpture, Yale University, New Haven, Connecticut
1981 The Architectural Association, London

Resides Spring Mills, Pennsylvania

***Challenge* exhibition** 1988

Selected solo exhibitions
1998 *Urban Oldfield,* Institute of Contemporary Art, Philadelphia
1996 *Charts,* Larry Becker Contemporary Art, Philadelphia
Watercourse, Rosenwald-Wolf Gallery, University of the Arts, Philadelphia
1995 *One Year in the Forest,* Pennsylvania State University, State College
1993 *A Month of Tides,* Wolfson Gallery, Miami-Dade Community College, Miami
1992 *Calendar of Rain,* Larry Becker Contemporary Art, Philadelphia
1991 *47 Feet into the Woods,* Abington Art Center, Jenkintown, Pennsylvania
Seeing the Path of the Wind, Levy Gallery for the Arts in Philadelphia, Moore College of Art and Design

Selected commissions
1996 *Cornerstones,* Eastlake neighborhood, Seattle
1994 Memorial for the Pennsylvania recipients of the Congressional Medal of Honor (with Winifred Lutz), Capitol Complex, Harrisburg

Selected group exhibitions
1996 *Arts Botanica,* Art in City Hall, Philadelphia
1994 *Objects and Souvenirs: Artist's Multiples,* Rosenwald-Wolf Gallery, University of the Arts, Philadelphia
1990 *Contemporary Philadelphia Artists: A Juried Exhibition,* Philadelphia Museum of Art

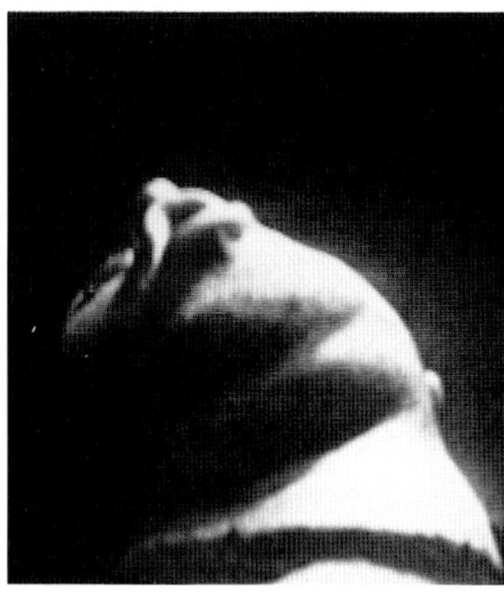

Tristin Lowe

Born
1966 Boston

Studied
1990 B.F.A. in sculpture, Massachusetts College of Art, Boston
1986 Fine art, Parsons School of Design, New York

Resides Philadelphia

***Challenge* exhibition** 1996

Selected solo exhibitions
1994 *September–Sleepy Hollow,* Vox Populi Gallery, Philadelphia
1992 *Balls and All,* Vox Populi Gallery, Philadelphia
1991 Hudson D. Walker Gallery at the Fine Arts Work Center, Provincetown, Massachusetts
1989 Thompson Gallery, Massachusetts College of Art, Boston

Selected group exhibitions
1997 *Objects and Souvenirs: Artist's Multiples,* Rosenwald-Wolf Gallery, University of the Arts, Philadelphia
1996 *You Talkin' to Me?,* Institute of Contemporary Art, Philadelphia
1995 *Philadelphia Selections I,* Levy Gallery for the Arts in Philadelphia, Moore College of Art and Design
   Specimens, Art in City Hall, Philadelphia

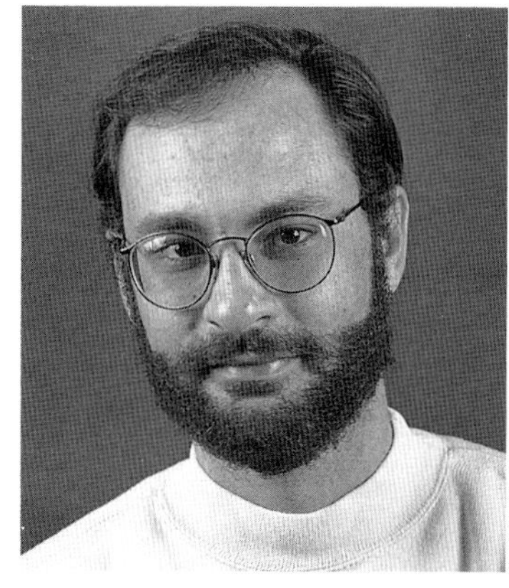

Gabriel Martinez

Born
1967 Miami

Studied
1991 M.F.A. in photography, Tyler School of Art, Temple University, Philadelphia
1989 B.F.A. in photography, University of Florida, Gainesville

Teaches Samuel S. Fleisher Art Memorial, Philadelphia
   University of the Arts, Philadelphia

Resides Philadelphia

***Challenge* exhibition** 1994

Selected performances
1997 *A Slice of Heaven,* Institute of Contemporary Art, Philadelphia
1996 *Especially for You,* Franklin Furnace, New York
1995 *100% Body Surface,* White Columns, New York; Nexus Foundation for Today's Art, Philadelphia
1994 *The Amusement Room* and *Body and Steel,* Samuel S. Fleisher Art Memorial, Philadelphia

Selected solo exhibitions
1998 *Dominion over Gentility,* Nexus Foundation for Today's Art, Philadelphia
1993 *Vanity,* The Booktrader Gallery, Philadelphia
1991 *Renaissance Series,* Temple Gallery, Temple University, Philadelphia

1989 *The Sensual, the Sexual, and the Pornographic,* Artitorium Gallery, Gainesville, Florida

Selected group exhibitions
1997 *Altered Egos,* Hallwalls Contemporary Arts Center, Buffalo
   Nexus Is 21, Nexus Foundation for Today's Art, Philadelphia
1996 *Complexity and Contradiction: Postmodernism in Philadelphia Photography,* Paley Design Center, Philadelphia College of Textiles and Science
   In the Flow: Alternate Authoring Strategies, Franklin Furnace, New York
   Private Acts and Earthly Delights, Nexus Foundation for Today's Art, Philadelphia
   The Strange Power of Cheap Sentiment (or A Bientôt to Irony), White Columns, New York
   You Talkin' to Me?, Institute of Contemporary Art, Philadelphia
   Works on Paper, Beaver College Art Gallery, Glenside, Pennsylvania
1995 *Flesh, Fetish, and Fashion: Three Activated Installations,* White Columns, New York
   The Nude: Beyond the Studio, Philadelphia Art Alliance
1994 *Objects and Souvenirs: Artist's Multiples,* Rosenwald-Wolf Gallery, University of the Arts, Philadelphia
1992 *Out and Exposed: New Works,* National Museum of Lesbian and Gay History, New York

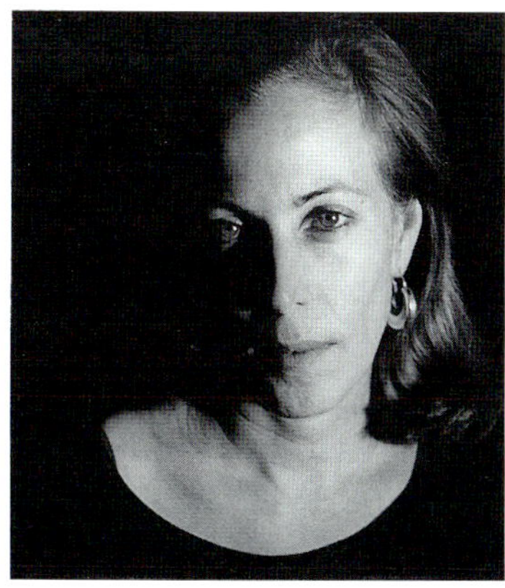

Susan Moore

Born
1953 Coco Solo, United States Canal Zone

Studied
1979 M.F.A. in painting, University of
California at Davis
1977 B.F.A. in painting, Indiana University,
Bloomington

Teaches Tyler School of Art, Temple
University, Philadelphia

Resides Philadelphia

Challenge exhibition 1982

Selected solo exhibitions
1995 Locks Gallery, Philadelphia
1992 Janet Fleisher Gallery, Philadelphia
1991 Morris Gallery, Pennsylvania
Academy of the Fine Arts, Philadelphia
1989 The More Gallery, Philadelphia
1987 Millersville University, Pennsylvania
1986 Tyler School of Art, Temple
University, Rome
1985 University of Michigan, Ann Arbor
1983 Timothy Burns Gallery, Saint Louis

Selected group exhibitions
1997 *Women Mentoring Women,* Westby Art
Gallery, Rowan University, Glassboro, New
Jersey
1990 *Contemporary Philadelphia Artists:
A Juried Exhibition,* Philadelphia Museum
of Art
1988 *163rd Annual Exhibition,* National
Academy of Design, New York
1987 *Selections 37,* The Drawing Center,
New York

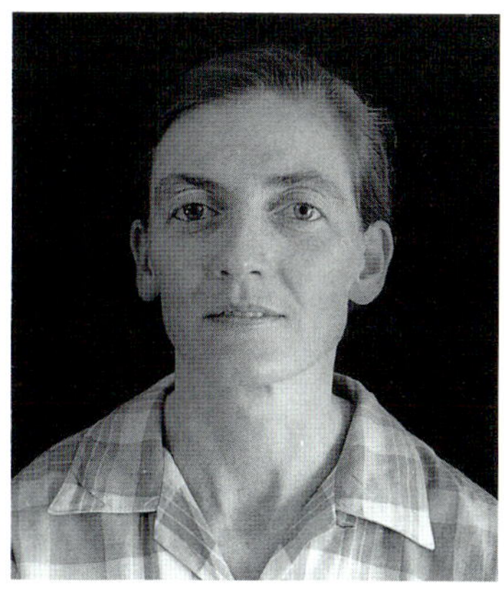

Kate Moran

Born
1958 Langhorne, Pennsylvania

Studied
1992 M.F.A. in visual arts, University of
North Carolina, Chapel Hill
1988 Certificate, Pennsylvania Academy of
the Fine Arts, Philadelphia
1982 B.A. in visual arts, Antioch College,
Yellow Springs, Ohio

Resides Philadelphia

Challenge exhibition 1992

Selected solo exhibitions
1998 *Vitreous Humours,* Morris Gallery,
Museum of American Art, Pennsylvania
Academy of the Fine Arts, Philadelphia
1997 *Emissaries,* List Gallery, Swarthmore
College, Pennsylvania
1996 *nine dolls full of color who understand
touch,* John Michael Kohler Arts Center,
Sheboygan, Wisconsin
1995 *The Grotesque and Ideal,* Williams
Center for the Arts, Lafayette College,
Easton, Pennsylvania
   Systemic Supports, The More Gallery,
Philadelphia
1994 *Recent Works,* The More Gallery,
Philadelphia
   Sculptural Works, Philadelphia Art Alliance
1993 *Acts of Delicacy,* Nexus Foundation for
Today's Art, Philadelphia
1992 *Fatigue,* Westby Art Gallery, Rowan
College, Glassboro, New Jersey

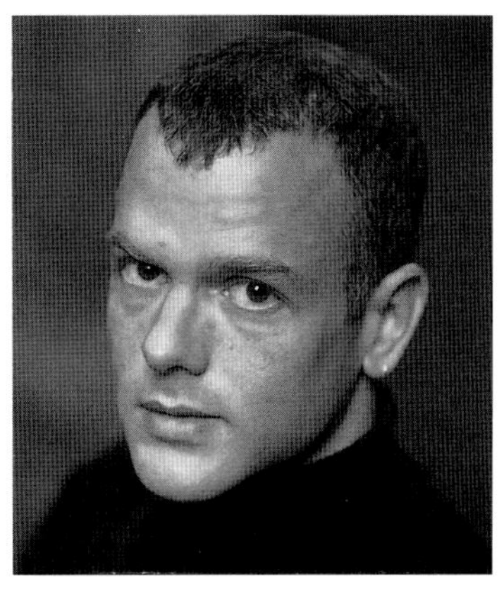

Brooke Moyer

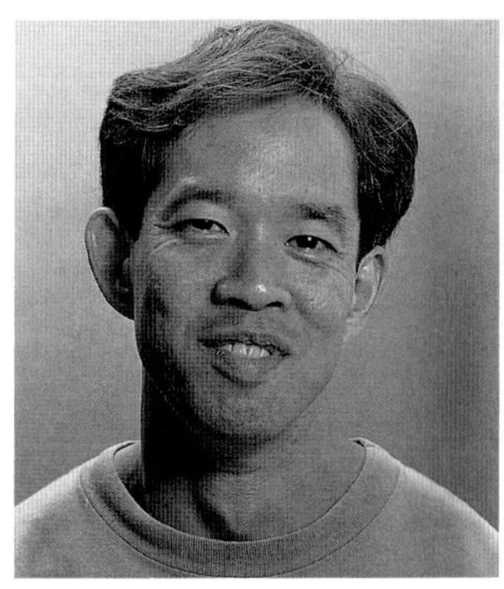

Don Nakamura

Selected group exhibitions
1997 *Hung Out to Dry*, Steinbaum Krauss Gallery, New York
1996 *Biennial '96*, Delaware Art Museum, Wilmington
Creative Artists Network: Selections, 1984–96, Woodmere Art Museum, Philadelphia
New Art on Paper 2: The Hunt Manufacturing Co. Collection, Philadelphia Museum of Art
Objects and Souvenirs: Artist's Multiples, Rosenwald-Wolf Gallery, University of the Arts, Philadelphia
Vestiges, Suzanne H. Arnold Art Gallery, Lebanon College of Pennsylvania, Annville
1995 *In Three Dimensions: Women Sculptors of the '90s,* Snug Harbor Cultural Center, Staten Island, New York

Born
1963 Doylestown, Pennsylvania

Studied
1993 M.F.A. in ceramics, Cranbrook Academy of Art, Bloomfield Hills, Michigan
1988 B.F.A. in ceramics, Philadelphia College of Art
1982–86 Industrial design, Philadelphia College of Art

Teaches Main Line Art Center, Haverford, Pennsylvania

Resides Philadelphia

***Challenge* exhibition** 1997

Selected solo exhibition
1996 Nexus Foundation for Today's Art, Philadelphia

Selected group exhibitions
1997 *Art of the State,* State Museum of Pennsylvania, Harrisburg
Nexus Is 21, Nexus Foundation for Today's Art, Philadelphia
1994 *Color Now,* Main Line Art Center, Haverford, Pennsylvania
1989 *The Body in Pain,* Forum Gallery, Cranbrook Academy of Art Museum, Bloomfield Hills, Michigan
1987 *Artists-in-Residence Show,* The Moravian Tile Works, Doylestown, Pennsylvania

Born
1955 Wailuku, Hawaii

Studied
1986 M.F.A. in ceramics, Cranbrook Academy of Art, Bloomfield Hills, Michigan
1984 B.F.A. in ceramics, Kansas City Art Institute, Missouri
1977 B.Ed. in music, University of Hawaii, Honolulu

Resides Philadelphia

***Challenge* exhibition** 1996

Selected solo exhibitions
1997–98 The Clay Studio, Philadelphia
1988 The Clay Studio, Philadelphia
1987 Art Department Gallery, Kent State University, Ohio

Selected group exhibitions
1998 *Biennial 1998,* Delaware Art Museum, Wilmington
1997 *Artistic Simplicity*, Pentimenti Gallery, Philadelphia
Pots '97, Chester Springs Studio, Pennsylvania
1996 *Art of the State*, State Museum of Pennsylvania, Harrisburg
1994 *Twentieth Anniversary Show*, The Clay Studio, Philadelphia

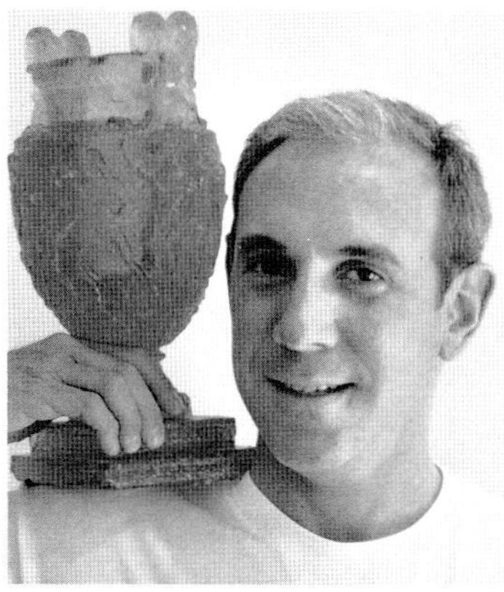

Stuart Netsky

Born
1955 Philadelphia

Studied
1990 M.F.A. in sculpture, Tyler School of
Art, Temple University, Philadelphia
1986 M.A. in sculpture and art education,
Philadelphia College of Art
1977 B.S. in design, Drexel University,
Philadelphia

Teaches Drexel University, Philadelphia
   Philadelphia College of Textiles and
Science
   University of the Arts, Philadelphia

Resides Philadelphia

Challenge exhibition 1991

Selected solo exhibitions
1997 Z Gallery, New York
1995 *New Sculpture and Paintings*, Larry
Becker Contemporary Art, Philadelphia
   Lipton Owens, New York
1993 *Time Flies*, Institute of Contemporary
Art, Philadelphia
1991 Nexus Foundation for Today's Art,
Philadelphia
1988 Gas Station, New York
   Nexus Foundation for Today's Art,
Philadelphia
1986 Philadelphia College of Art

Selected group exhibitions
1997 *Art of the Matter,* Mason Gross School
of the Arts, Rutgers University, New
Brunswick, New Jersey
   Domestic Diversions, Philadelphia Art
Alliance
1996 *Brenda and Other Stories,* Walsall
Museum and Art Gallery, England
   Model Home, Clocktower Gallery, New
York
   Patterns of Excess, Beaver College Art
Gallery, Glenside, Pennsylvania
   Private Acts and Earthly Delights, Nexus
Foundation for Today's Art, Philadelphia
   Self-Possessed, Lubbock Fine Arts Center,
Texas
1995 *Faggots: A Communiqué from North
America*, Fundación Rojas, University of
Buenos Aires
   Strictly Personal, Delaware Center for the
Contemporary Arts, Wilmington
1994 *Objects and Souvenirs: Artist's
Multiples,* Rosenwald-Wolf Gallery,
University of the Arts, Philadelphia
   Social Fabric, Beaver College Art Gallery,
Glenside, Pennsylvania
   Stonewall, White Columns, New York
1993 *Dress Codes,* Institute of Contem-
porary Art, Boston
1992 *Shams,* Fabric Workshop,
Philadelphia
   The Temporal Image: A Farewell to Frills,
Momenta Art, Philadelphia
   Utopia/Dystopia, The Print Club,
Philadelphia
1991 *Good Housekeeping,* Levy Gallery for
the Arts in Philadelphia, Moore College of
Art and Design

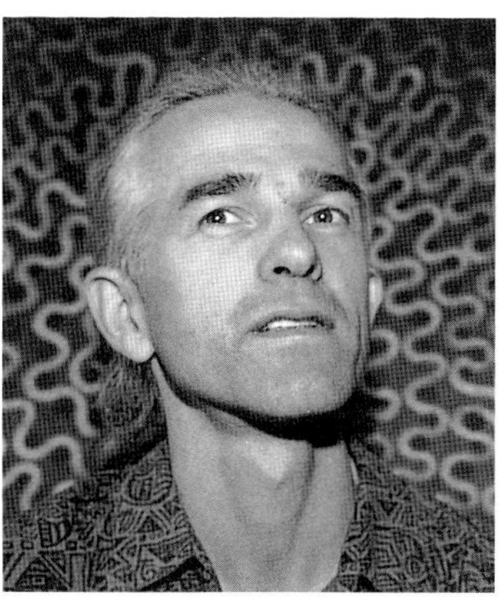

Bruce Pollock

Born
1951 Painesville, Ohio

Studied
1978 M.F.A. in painting, Tyler School of
Art, Temple University, Philadelphia
1976–77 Tyler School of Art, Temple
University, Rome
1976 B.F.A. in painting, Cleveland School
of Art
1970–71 Carnegie Mellon University,
Pittsburgh

Teaches Drexel University, Philadelphia

Resides Philadelphia

Challenge exhibition 1979

Selected solo exhibitions
1995 Janet Fleisher Gallery, Philadelphia
1991 Janet Fleisher Gallery, Philadelphia
1990 Design Arts Gallery, Nesbitt College
of Design Arts, Drexel University,
Philadelphia
   Morris Gallery, Pennsylvania Academy
of the Fine Arts, Philadelphia
1987 Janet Fleisher Gallery, Philadelphia
1986 Cavin-Morris, Inc., New York
1984 Laurence Miller Gallery, New York
   Jeffrey Fuller Fine Art, Philadelphia
1982 Alan Stone Gallery, New York
   Jeffrey Fuller Fine Art, Philadelphia
   Karen Lennox Gallery, Chicago
1981 Dome Room Gallery, New
Educational Center for the Arts, New
Haven, Connecticut

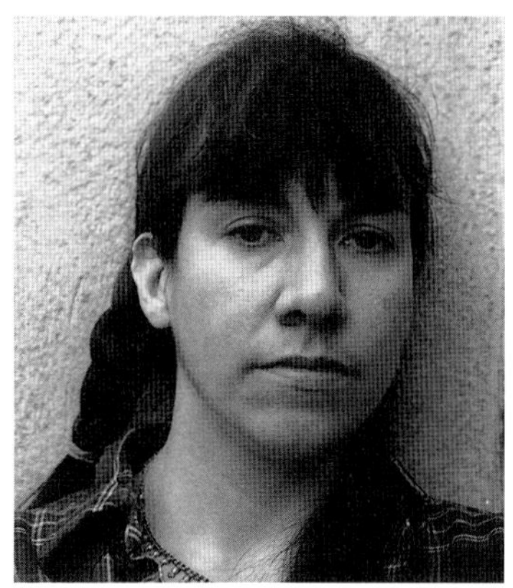

Judith Schaechter

Selected group exhibitions
1997 *Abstract Strategies,* Philadelphia Art Alliance
1996 *Biennial '96,* Delaware Art Museum, Wilmington
1995 *Prison Sentences: The Prison Site/The Prison as Subject,* Eastern State Penitentiary, Philadelphia
1992 *Pertaining to Philadelphia: Contemporary Acquisitions from the Julius Bloch Memorial Fund,* Philadelphia Museum of Art
1990 *Contemporary Philadelphia Artists: A Juried Exhibition,* Philadelphia Museum of Art
1987 *Made in Philadelphia,* Institute of Contemporary Art, Philadelphia
1979 *Summer at the Morris Gallery,* Morris Gallery, Pennsylvania Academy of the Fine Arts, Philadelphia

Born
1961 Gainesville, Florida

Studied
1983 B.F.A. in sculpture (Glass Program), Rhode Island School of Design, Providence

Teaches Pennsylvania Academy of the Fine Arts, Philadelphia
University of the Arts, Philadelphia

Resides Philadelphia

***Challenge* exhibition** 1990

Selected solo exhibitions
1997 *New Work,* Snyderman Gallery, Philadelphia
1996 Cincinnati Art Center
1995 *Heart Attacks: Judith Schaechter,* Institute of Contemporary Art, Philadelphia
John Michael Kohler Arts Center, Sheboygan, Wisconsin
1994 *Recent Work,* Snyderman Gallery, Philadelphia
1993 Helander Gallery, New York; Palm Beach, Florida
1992 *Virtue Triumphs,* Le Luz de Jesus Gallery, Los Angeles
1991 Snyderman Gallery, Philadelphia
1988 *Beckoning Graves,* Nexus Foundation for Today's Art, Philadelphia
1984 Nexus Foundation for Today's Art, Philadelphia

Selected group exhibitions
1998 *Biennial 1998,* Delaware Art Museum, Wilmington
1997 *The Varieties of Religious Experience,* Painted Bride Art Center, Philadelphia
1992 *American Crafts: The Nation's Collection,* Renwick Gallery, National Museum of American Art, Smithsonian Institution, Washington, D.C.
Treasures from the Corning Museum, Yokohama Museum, Japan
1991 *Artist of Conscience,* Alternative Museum, New York
1990 *Contemporary Philadelphia Artists: A Juried Exhibition,* Philadelphia Museum of Art

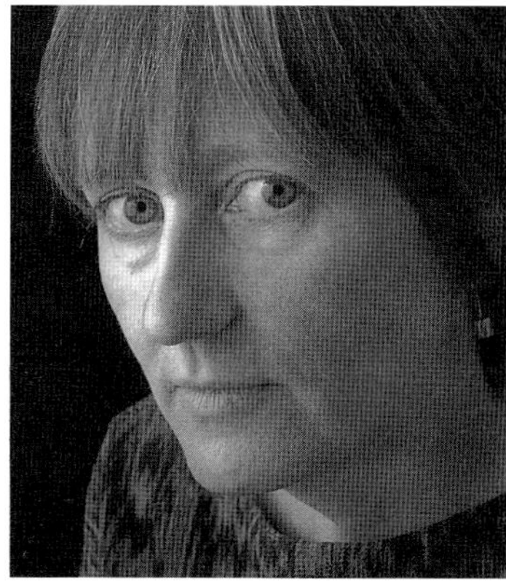

Hester Stinnett

Born
1956 Baltimore

Studied
1982 M.F.A. in printmaking, Tyler School
of Art, Temple University, Philadelphia
1978 B.F.A. in printmaking, Hartford
Art School, University of Hartford,
Connecticut

Teaches Tyler School of Art, Temple
University, Philadelphia

Resides Philadelphia

Challenge exhibition 1982

Selected solo exhibitions
1988 *Improvisational Woodcuts,*
Dolan/Maxwell Gallery, Philadelphia
1986 Comfort Gallery, Haverford,
Pennsylvania
1985 Burke Hall Art Gallery, Denison
University, Granville, Ohio

Selected group exhibitions
1997–98 *Abstract Strategies,* Philadelphia
Art Alliance
1996 *Biennial '96,* Delaware Art Museum,
Wilmington
   Four Printmakers, Wilson Gallery,
Rowan College, Glassboro, New Jersey
1994 *Works on Paper,* Beaver College Art
Gallery, Glenside, Pennsylvania
1993 *Diverse Works: Ten Years of Printmaking at the Brandywine Workshop*
(organized by the United States Information Agency), traveled throughout Brazil
1992 *Pertaining to Philadelphia: Contemporary Acquisitions from the Julius Bloch
Memorial Fund*, Philadelphia Museum
of Art

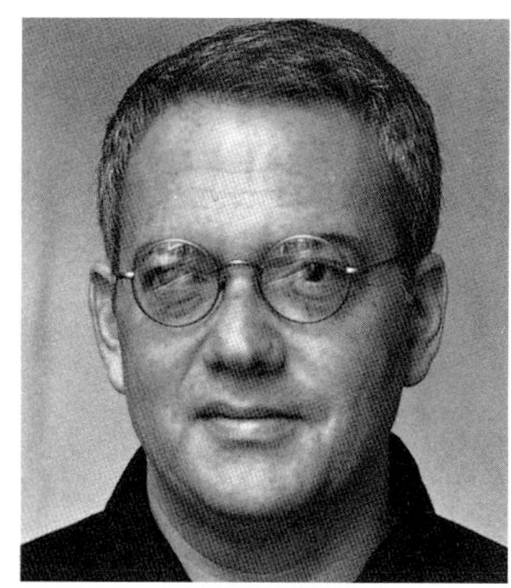

Stephen Talasnik

Born
1954 Philadelphia

Studied
1979 M.F.A. in painting, Tyler School of
Art, Temple University, Philadelphia
1977–78 Tyler School of Art, Temple
University, Rome
1976–77 Syracuse University, New York
1976 B.F.A. in painting, Rhode Island
School of Design, Providence

Resides New York

Challenge exhibition 1980

Selected solo exhibitions
1998 *Small Works on Paper,* Marsha
Mateyka Gallery, Washington, D.C.
   Visionary Objects, Panoramas, and Maps,
American Architectural Foundation,
American Institute of Architects Head-
quarters Gallery, Washington, D.C.
1996 *New Fossils,* Inform Gallery, Kana-
zawa, Japan
1995 *Drawings: 1990–1994,* Weatherspoon
Art Gallery, University of North Carolina,
Greensboro
   Recent Manuscripts, Davidson Galleries,
Seattle

1994 *Recent Work,* Schmidt/Dean Gallery, Philadelphia

Visionary Projects, Van Rooy Galerie, Amsterdam

1993 *Visionary Shrines,* Inform Gallery, Kanazawa, Japan

1990 *Recent Drawings,* Dolan/Maxwell Gallery, New York

1988 *Japan Drawings,* Dolan/Maxwell Gallery, Philadelphia

1987 *Mythology: Recent Drawings,* Morris Gallery, Pennsylvania Academy of the Fine Arts, Philadelphia

1985 Janet Fleisher Gallery, Philadelphia
Bryce Gallery, Moore College of Art and Design, Philadelphia

1984 *Recent Artifacts,* DuBois Art Gallery, Lehigh University, Bethlehem, Pennsylvania

1983 Philadelphia Art Alliance
Janet Fleisher Gallery, Philadelphia

1981 Rosemont College, Pennsylvania

1980 *Drawing and Burial Artifacts,* Stockton State College, Pomona, New Jersey

Selected group exhibitions

1998 *Drawing Acquisitions,* Graphische Sammlung Albertina, Vienna

1997 *Recent Drawing Acquisitions,* Teylers Museum, Haarlem, The Netherlands
Stung by Splendor: Working Drawings and the Creative Moment, Houghton Gallery, Cooper Union, New York

1996 *Recent Acquisitions: Drawings and Prints,* The British Museum, London
Structural Foundations of Clarity, Arkansas Art Center, Little Rock

1993 *Karuizawa International Drawing Biennial,* Wakita Museum of Art, Karuizawa, Japan

1992 *Vessels for Discovery,* Islip Art Museum, New York

1991 *Recent Acquisitions,* National Museum of American Art, Smithsonian Institution, Washington, D.C.
Works on Paper: Recent Acquisitions, Brooklyn Museum, New York

1990 *Works on Paper: Contemporary American Drawing,* High Museum of Art, Atlanta

1988 *Achromatic Variations,* Levy Gallery for the Arts in Philadelphia, Moore College of Art and Design

1984 *Selections 27,* The Drawing Center, New York

1979 *Small Works on Paper,* Newcastle Polytechnic, England

Lisa Bartolozzi

1. *Tell Us About Magdelene*, 1993
Oil on panel
14½ × 16½" (36.8 × 41.9 cm)
Collection of the artist

2. *The Marking of Foreheads*, 1994
Oil, ink, and wax on panel
9½ × 17 × 3¼" (24.1 × 43.2 × 8.2 cm)
Collection of Leslie Cecil and
Creighton Michael

3. *Model*, 1997
Oil on panel
10 × 8" (25.4 × 20.3 cm) image
Collection of Mr. and Mrs. E.
Hatchadoorian
PLATE 1

Lanny Bergner

4. *Untitled*, 1988
Charcoal on paper
54½ × 25¼" (138.4 × 64.1 cm)
Philadelphia Museum of Art. Gift of
Diane and Martin Greitzer. 1989-7-1

5. *Dark Twist III*, 1989
Screen and aluminum wire
96 × 12 × 12" (243.8 × 30.5 × 30.5 cm)
Collection of Ned and Kathy Putnam

6. *Being Forest*, 1997
Screen, monofilament, and copper wire
35 × 15 × 15" (88.9 × 38.1 × 38.1 cm)
Collection of the artist
PLATE 2

Norinne Betjemann

7. *Freefall,* 1989
Photo oils and gold leaf on gelatin silver
print (second from an edition of five)
59 × 38" (149.9 × 96.5 cm)
Collection of Norma and Lawrence
Reichlin
PLATE 3

8. *Amulet*, 1992
Photo oils and gold leaf on gelatin silver
print
53¼ × 39¾" (135.2 × 101 cm)
Collection of James D. Crawford and
Judith N. Dean

9. *Foxglove*, 1995
Acrylic on patched gelatin silver prints,
mounted on canvas
60 × 41" (152.4 × 104.1 cm)
Collection of James D. Crawford and
Judith N. Dean

Charles Burwell

10. *Internal-External Structure II*, 1989
Watercolor, oil, and crayon on paper
40 × 38" (101.6 × 96.5 cm)
Collection of First Union National Bank,
Philadelphia

11. *Internal-External Structure III*, 1989
Oil stick and crayon on paper
28¾ × 30⅛" (73 × 76.5 cm)
Collection of Leonard and Nancy
Amoroso

12. *Broken Labyrinth #5*, 1997
Watercolor, graphite, pastel, ink, and tempera on paper
50 × 36" (127 × 91.4 cm)
Collection of the artist, courtesy Sande Webster Gallery, Philadelphia

13. *Broken Labyrinth #8, Hybrids*, 1997
Watercolor, graphite, pastel, ink, and tempera on paper
50 × 32" (127 × 81.3 cm)
Collection of the artist, courtesy Sande Webster Gallery, Philadelphia
PLATE 4

Syd Carpenter

14. *Familiar Figure*, 1991
Acrylic on earthenware
53 × 24 × 9" (134.6 × 61 × 22.9 cm)
Collection of R. A. Ellison

15. *Still Processing*, 1994
Acrylic on earthenware with stones, painted wood brush, and plaster
50 × 18 × 10" (127 × 45.7 × 25.4 cm)
Collection of the artist, courtesy Sande Webster Gallery, Philadelphia
PLATE 5

16. *Woman Overboard*, 1998
Acrylic on earthenware
16 × 30 × 28" (40.6 × 76.2 × 71.1 cm)
Collection of the artist, courtesy Sande Webster Gallery, Philadelphia

Frank Galuszka

17. *Bethany*, 1979–82
Oil on canvas
102 × 80¾" (259.1 × 205.1 cm)
Collection of the artist, courtesy The More Gallery, Inc., Philadelphia
PLATE 6

18. *Into the Earth*, 1992
Oil, acrylic, gold leaf, Shiny Stuff, paper, Kodak film box, and sawdust on canvas
84 × 68" (213.4 × 172.7 cm)
Collection of the artist, courtesy The More Gallery, Inc., Philadelphia

Michael Grothusen

19. *Moving the Museum*, an installation on the East Balcony of the Great Stair Hall of the Philadelphia Museum of Art, 1998
See PLATE 7

Mei-ling Hom

20. *Golden Mountain*, an installation in the American Wing (Gallery 119) of the Philadelphia Museum of Art, 1998
See PLATE 8

Stacy Levy

21. *Hidden River*, 1990
Galvanized pipe, porcelain sinks, water, sandblasted glass, PVC pipe, vinyl letters, and water pump
15 × 30 × 2½' (4.6 × 9.1 × 0.8 m)
Courtesy Fairmount Water Works Interpretive Center, Philadelphia Water Department
PLATE 9

Tristin Lowe

22. *Alice*, an installation in the twentieth-century galleries (Gallery 178) of the Philadelphia Museum of Art, 1998
See PLATE 10

Gabriel Martinez

23. *Anterior Torso and Facial Features*, 1994
Duratrans display material in light box
72 × 48 × 12" (182.9 × 121.9 × 30.5 cm)
Collection of the artist
FIGURE 12

24. *Self-Portraits by Heterosexual Men*, 1996–98
Ambrotypes, mounted in nineteenth-century brass frames with velvet and mahogany (series of 100)
3⅛ × 2¾" (7.9 × 7 cm) each
Collection of the artist
See PLATE 11

Susan Moore

25. *Untitled*, 1981
Oil on canvas
14⅛ × 11" (35.9 × 27.9 cm)
Private collection

26. *Untitled*, 1981
Oil on canvas
14⅛ × 11" (35.9 × 27.9 cm)
Collection of Steven Levin and Aida Laleian

27. *Untitled*, 1981
Oil on canvas
14⅛ × 11" (35.9 × 27.9 cm)
Collection of Kimber and Jeff Michels

28. *Back Portraits*, 1995
Oil on canvas
32 × 20" (81.3 × 50.8 cm) each
Courtesy Locks Gallery, Philadelphia
PLATE 12

29. *Back Portraits*, 1995
Oil on canvas
32 × 20" (81.3 × 50.8 cm)
Courtesy Locks Gallery, Philadelphia

Kate Moran

30. *Saying and devouring it,* 1993
Hand-colored and manipulated
silver prints (series of three)
48 × 24" (121.9 × 61 cm) each
Collection of the artist
PLATE 13

31. *Untitled,* from *nine dolls full of color
who understand touch,* 1994
Cast wax, fabric body, and wood chair
(two from a series of nine)
22½ × 7 × 9½" (57.1 × 17.8 × 24.1 cm)
14½ × 6 × 8" (36.8 × 15.2 × 20.3 cm)
Collection of the artist

Brooke Moyer

32. *Men-an-tol,* 1996
Epoxy resin, fiberglass, and pigmented
varnish
43 × 44 × 6½" (109.2 × 111.8 × 16.5 cm)
Collection of Douglas Smith
PLATE 14

33. *More,* 1996
Epoxy resin, fiberglass, and aluminum
leaf
54 × 72" (137.2 × 182.9 cm)
Collection of Douglas Smith

Don Nakamura

34. *My Space,* 1996
Low-fire glazes on earthenware and wire
68 × 43 × 75" (172.7 × 109.2 × 190.5 cm)
Collection of the artist
PLATE 15

Stuart Netsky

35. *Monet's Haystacks,* 1988
Plastic billboard flickers on plastic,
mounted on wood
78½ × 117½" (199.4 × 298.4 cm)
Collection of the artist, courtesy Larry
Becker Contemporary Art, Philadelphia
PLATE 16

36. *Monet's Water Lilies,* 1988
Plastic billboard flickers on plastic,
mounted on wood
68½ × 137½" (174 × 349.2 cm)
Collection of the artist, courtesy Larry
Becker Contemporary Art, Philadelphia

37. *Untitled,* 1997
Lipstick on panel
6 × 6" (15.2 × 15.2 cm)
Collection of the artist, courtesy Larry
Becker Contemporary Art, Philadelphia

38. *Untitled,* 1997
Lipstick on panel
6 × 6" (15.2 × 15.2 cm)
Collection of the artist, courtesy Larry
Becker Contemporary Art, Philadelphia

39. *Untitled,* 1997
Lipstick on panel
6 × 6" (15.2 × 15.2 cm)
Collection of the artist, courtesy Larry
Becker Contemporary Art, Philadelphia

40. *Untitled,* 1998
Nail enamel and powdered pigment
on linen
22 × 28" (55.9 × 71.1 cm)
Collection of the artist, courtesy Larry
Becker Contemporary Art, Philadelphia

Bruce Pollock

41. *Bangor,* 1979
Enamel on pine
6½ × 5 × 6" (16.5 × 12.7 × 15.2 cm)
Philadelphia Museum of Art. Julius
Bloch Memorial Fund. 1981-43-3

42. *Dauphin,* 1979
Enamel on pine
5¾ × 6½ × 7" (14.6 × 16.5 × 17.8 cm)
Philadelphia Museum of Art. Julius
Bloch Memorial Fund. 1981-43-2

43. *Duplex,* 1980
Enamel on pine
6⅜ × 6⅛ × 7¹/₁₆" (16.2 × 15.5 × 17.9 cm)
Philadelphia Museum of Art. Julius
Bloch Memorial Fund. 1981-43-4

44. *Lennox,* 1980
Enamel on pine
5¾ × 6¾ × 7⅛" (14.6 × 17.1 × 18.1 cm)
Philadelphia Museum of Art. Julius
Bloch Memorial Fund. 1981-43-1

45. *Trenton,* 1980
Enamel on pine
6¼ × 6 × 7¾" (15.9 × 15.2 × 19.7 cm)
Philadelphia Museum of Art. Julius
Bloch Memorial Fund. 1981-43-5

46. *Net of Indra,* 1997
Oil on canvas
70 × 60" (177.8 × 152.4 cm)
Courtesy Fleisher/Ollman Gallery,
Philadelphia
PLATE 17

Judith Schaechter

47. *When the Hunter Sings the Birds
Take Wing*, 1991
Stained glass
20 × 26" (50.8 × 66 cm)
Private collection

48. *I've Trampled a Million Pretty
Flowers*, 1995
Stained glass
47 × 21" (119.4 × 53.3 cm)
Philadelphia Museum of Art. Gift of the
Women's Committee of the Philadelphia
Museum of Art. 1995-81-2
PLATE 18

Hester Stinnett

49. *Monoprint #13*, 1987
Monoprint
37¾ × 38¼" (95.9 × 97.1 cm)
Philadelphia Museum of Art. Julius
Bloch Memorial Fund. 1988-20-1

50. *#115*, 1996
Suminagashi, woodblock, and screen print
36 × 27" (91.4 × 68.6 cm)
Collection of the artist

51. *#127*, 1997
Suminagashi, woodblock, and screen print
36 × 27" (91.4 × 68.6 cm)
Collection of the artist
PLATE 19

Stephen Talasnik

52. *Burial Collar #2*, 1982
Graphite and Conté crayon on paper
37 × 37" (94 × 94 cm)
Collection of James D. Crawford and
Judith N. Dean

53. *Visionary Objects: Implant, Beacon,
Split,* and *Pinch*, 1997
Graphite on paper
22 × 17" (55.9 × 43.2 cm) each
Collection of the artist *(Implant,
Beacon, Pinch)*
Collection of Sydnee and Seymour
Martin Lipset *(Split)*
PLATE 20

FLEISHER *CHALLENGE*
EXHIBITIONS, 1978–98

1978–79

CHALLENGE 1

Frank Galuszka*
Lucy Glick
Mary Sentner Nicol

CHALLENGE 2

Frieda Fehrenbacher*
Barry Lehr
Michael Williamson

CHALLENGE 3

Kathy Halton*
Larry Spaid*
Ruth Wolf*

CHALLENGE 4

Anita C. Harris
Diane Pieri*
Bruce Pollock*

Jurors Sam Maitin
John Moore
Jody Pinto

1979–80

CHALLENGE 1

Lydia Hunn*
Jan Morgen*
Rosalie Sherman*

CHALLENGE 2

Barbara Danin*
Leonard Han
Stephanie Tyiska

CHALLENGE 3

Hillary Reehl
Richard Rothrock*
Stephen Talasnik*

CHALLENGE 4

Rosemarie Certo
Gail Gosser*
Mary Ann Krutsick*

Jurors Ruth Fine
Ben Kamihira
Phillips Simkin
Judith Steinhauser
Ken Vavrek

1980–81

CHALLENGE 1

Thom Bell-Games
Georgette L. Veeder*
Michael D. Willse*

CHALLENGE 2

Judith Brodie*
William Scott Noel*
Dan Wittels*

CHALLENGE 3

Richard Ciocco*
Felix Giordano*
Ruth Locke Selzer*

CHALLENGE 4

Jeffrey Boys*
Frances Storey*
John E. Troy

*Included in the exhibition *20 × 12:
A Generation of "Challenge" Artists*,
at the Samuel S. Fleisher Art Memorial,
Philadelphia (July 18–August 28, 1998).

Jurors Harry Anderson
Ron Bateman
Lois Johnson
Jack Thompson

1981–82

CHALLENGE 1

Clarisse Carnell
Joyce Fillip
James Rauchman

CHALLENGE 2

Sue Brandon*
Ed Collins
Dennis E. Congdon

CHALLENGE 3

Michael Garrity*
Mel Leipzig*
Susan Moore*

CHALLENGE 4

Jon F. Clark*
Brian A. Meunier*
Sid Sachs

Jurors Charles Fahlen
Sidney Goodman
David Pease
Paula Winokur
Becky Young

1982–83

CHALLENGE 1

John J. Carlano*
Tom Ferris*
Susan Chrysler White

CHALLENGE 2

Sam-Karen Norgard*
Hester Stinnett*
William Welch

CHALLENGE 3

Marilyn Ashbrook*
Peter Grimord*
Robert C. Rotella

CHALLENGE 4

Richard Hricko*
Babette Martino*
Scott M. Roper

Jurors Edna Andrade
Laurence Bach
John Dowell
Sue-Yun Pyo
Bruce Samuelson
Warren Seelig

1983–84

CHALLENGE 1

Linda Besemer*
Richard Sanders*
Evan David Summer*

CHALLENGE 2

Yarrott Benz
Tom Levy*
James L. McElhinney*

CHALLENGE 3

Warren Angle*
Martha Vaughn*
Irwin Weiss

CHALLENGE 4

Robert Bingham*
Mark Campbell*
Perky Edgerton*

Jurors John Carnell
Bill Freeland
Lois Johnson
John Moore

1984–85

CHALLENGE 1

Lanny Bergner*
M. W. Burns
Dean Dass

CHALLENGE 2

Mark Kobasz*
Timothy Tracz*
Jo Spohn Yarrington*

CHALLENGE 3

Charles Burwell*
Rebecca Johnson
Francisco Perez

CHALLENGE 4

Elissa Glassgold
Arline Peco
Bruce West*

Jurors Frank Galuszka
Anthony Gorny
Winifred Lutz
William Earle Williams

1985–86

CHALLENGE 1

Jeffrey M. Blake
Marjorie S. Gapp*
Sarah McEneaney*

CHALLENGE 2

Anthony Ciambella*
Bruce G. Hanson
Robert Wurster

CHALLENGE 3

Richard Jordan*
Paul Runyon*
Bill Scott*

CHALLENGE 4
Thomas Durnell*
David Goerk
Teresa L. Jaynes*

Jurors Nancy Hellebrand
Maurie Kerrigan
Doris Staffel
Rochelle Toner

1986–87
CHALLENGE 1
Donna Bullard*
Patricia McCabe
Sarah Van Keuren*

CHALLENGE 2
Susan M. Haerry
Daniel F. Loewenstein
Mark McCullen*

CHALLENGE 3
Thomas Dan*
Margaretta Gilboy*
Therese Rolland*

CHALLENGE 4
Margery Amdur
Shelley Bachman
Julia Thompson

Jurors Moe Brooker
Larry Day
Judith Joy Ross
Phillips Simkin

1987–88
CHALLENGE 1
Sean Nixon*
Rick A. Ortwein*
Ann Reichlin

CHALLENGE 2
Janet Biggs
David Cann
Marty Fumo*

CHALLENGE 3
Emil A. Mellow II*
John Steele
Christina Yocca*

CHALLENGE 4
Peter Miraglia*
Kim Tieger
Peter Tong Xiao

Jurors Phoebe Adams
David Hannah
Sandra Lerner
Emily Medvec

1988–89
CHALLENGE 1
Norinne Betjemann*
Bonnie Levinthal*
Stacy Levy*

CHALLENGE 2
Elizabeth Brandt*
Phillip Donovan*
David Wyzenbeek

CHALLENGE 3
Colby Beutel
Michael Criston*
Roger Laib*

CHALLENGE 4
Stuart Rome*
Bryan Whitney
Kay Wood*

Jurors Martha Chahroudi
Tom Chimes
Paolo Columbo
David Lebe
Ann Percy
Jody Pinto
Mark Rosenthal
Darrel Sewell

1989–90
CHALLENGE 1
Robert Asman*
Susan Lowry
Mitchell Messina*

CHALLENGE 2
Timothy Aubry*
Irena Kononova*
Ken Mabrey*

CHALLENGE 3
Robert Moss-Vreeland
Judith Taylor*
Ann Hopkins Wilson*

CHALLENGE 4
Syd Carpenter*
Nicholas Kripal*
Judith Schaechter*

Jurors Adela Akers
Penny Bach
Martha Chahroudi
Alida Fish
Ellen Jacobowitz
Edith Neff
Ann Temkin
Stanley Whitney

1990–91

CHALLENGE 1

Marilyn Keating
Jane Marshall*
David K. A. Mohallatee

CHALLENGE 2

Neysa Grassi
Gary Owen Pelkey*
Jaimie Watson

CHALLENGE 3

John J. H. Phillip*
Annabeth Rosen*
Michael S. Smith*

CHALLENGE 4

Matthew Lawrence*
Elyse Saperstein*
Hinda Schuman*

CHALLENGE 5

Janet Grau
Jack Wax*
Graydon Wood*

Jurors Julie Courtney
Jerry Crimmins
Robert Keyser
Paula Marincola
Ann Percy
Darrel Sewell
Hester Stinnett
Ann Temkin
John Weiss
Paula Winokur

1991–92

CHALLENGE 1

Mei-ling Hom*
Todd Noe*
Stuart Shils*

CHALLENGE 2

Howard Brunner*
Selena Fitanides
Vincent Leon Olmsted

CHALLENGE 3

Lynne Allen*
Sandra Brownlee-Ramsdale*
Catherine Murray*

CHALLENGE 4

Barbara Grant*
James Mills
Scott Nyerick*

CHALLENGE 5

Stuart Netsky*
Gordon R. Smith*
Elizabeth Lee Wilkinson*

Jurors Dilys Blum
Yvonne Bobrowicz
Diane Burko
Martha Chahroudi
Jonas Dos Santos
John Ittmann
Ray Metzker
Patrick Murphy
Tony Rosati
Ann Temkin

1992–93

CHALLENGE 1

Ronald Abram
Michael Grothusen*
Kurt Rosenquist*

CHALLENGE 2

Harry Lynn Krizan*
Kate Moran*
Denyse Thomasos*

CHALLENGE 3

Jeanne Jaffe*
Miriam Wold
David G. Wright*

CHALLENGE 4

Sarah Slavick*
Sandy Sorlien*
Ron Wyffels*

Jurors Martha Chahroudi
William Daley
George Krause
Ann Percy
John Ravenal
Charles Searles
Darrel Sewell
Evan David Summer
Ann Temkin
Susan Chrysler White

1993–94

CHALLENGE 1

Christine Blair*
Christopher Giglio
Jeffrey Reed*

CHALLENGE 2

Fritz Dietel*
Rochelle Dinkin*
Lisa Michel Naples*

CHALLENGE 3

Hank Jaffe
Leah Reynolds*
Paul D. Santoleri*

CHALLENGE 4

Lisa Bartolozzi*
John Boyce*
Alan Greenberg*

Jurors Dilys Blum
Anne Fabbri
John Ittmann
Ray King
Paula Marincola
Hitoshi Nakazato
Eileen Neff
Diane Pieri
John Ravenal
Isaac Witkin

1994–95

CHALLENGE 1

Gabriel Martinez*
Jeffrey L. Peezick*
Gregory Tobias*

CHALLENGE 2

Stacy Collingham*
Joy Saville
Paul Sheehan*

CHALLENGE 3

Hilary Harp*
Virgil Marti*
Christopher Ransom*

CHALLENGE 4

William Cromar*
Mary Murphy*
Jennie Shanker*

Jurors Martha Chahroudi
Don Desmett
Anda Dubinskis
Melissa Feldman
David Graham
Susan Moore
Ann Percy
Darrel Sewell
Bill Walton
Robert Winokur

1995–96

CHALLENGE 1

Linda Lorrie Gross*
Mel Prest
Krista Van Ness*

CHALLENGE 2

Matthew Clowney*
Jo Owens*
James Rose*

CHALLENGE 3

Cris Larson*
Karen Rodewald*
William Smith*

CHALLENGE 4

Gretchen Hupfel*
Tristin Lowe*
Andrew Ross Wrigley*

Jurors Alice O. Beamesderfer
Yvonne Bobrowicz
James Clark
John Dowell
Kathleen Edwards
Homer Jackson
John Ravenal
Innis Howe Shoemaker
Judith Steinhauser
Stephen Talasnik

1996–97

CHALLENGE 1

Brian Coleman*
Barbara Klein*
Sandi Pierantozzi*

CHALLENGE 2

Hyejin Chung
Christine Lafuente*
Don Nakamura*

CHALLENGE 3

Gil Kerlin*
Michael Kowbuz*
Scott McMahon

CHALLENGE 4

Thomas Gartside*
Richard Harrod*
Andrea Zemel*

Jurors Penny Bach
Berrisford Boothe
Susan Fenton
Sidney Goodman
Ann Percy
Steven Perloff
Darrel Sewell
Ann Temkin
Richard Torchia
Paula Winokur

1997–98

CHALLENGE 1

Scott Finch*
Michael Lynn*
Ron Tarver*

CHALLENGE 2

Mark Goodwin*
Brooke Moyer*
Chris Mueller*

CHALLENGE 3

Jennifer Baker*
Mark Lueders*
Timi Sullivan*

CHALLENGE 4

Susan Lincoln Hockaday*
Anna Kuo*
Cynthia Porter*

Jurors Phoebe Adams
Lynn Denton
Anne Fabbri
John Ittmann
Lisa Panzera
Peter Paone
John Ravenal
Judith Tannenbaum
Willie Williams
Bhakti Ziek

All photographs courtesy the artist except as noted:

Warren Angle: figures 20, 21

Dennis Cowley: plate 20

Jeff Hurwitz: plate 19

Joe Painter: plate 9

Lynn Rosenthal: plate 18

Stephen Talasnik: figure 17

Graydon Wood: cover, frontispiece,
    figures 14, 16, 18, plates 1–8, 10–17

BIOGRAPHY PHOTOGRAPHS

Lisa Bartolozzi: Duane Perry

Charles Burwell: Dawoud Bey

Syd Carpenter: Steven Donegan

Frank Galuszka: Don Harris

Michael Grothusen: Nancy McDonald

Stacy Levy: Heidi Nivling, courtesy Larry Becker
    Contemporary Art, Philadelphia

Gabriel Martinez: Karen Rodenwald

Susan Moore: Rosalyn Duffy

Kate Moran: Thomas Gartside

Brooke Moyer: Ken Yanokiak

Don Nakamura: Jack Ramsdale

Stuart Netsky: Heidi Nivling, courtesy Larry Becker
    Contemporary Art, Philadelphia

Bruce Pollock: Stuart Rome

Judith Schaechter: Courtesy Snyderman Gallery,
    Philadelphia

Hester Stinnett: Jeff Hurwitz

Stephen Talasnik: B. Kaufman